Contents Guide

Section 1: Introduction

1. Welcome & What You'll Learn
2. Unveiling Splunk: Your Gateway to Data Empowerment

Section 2: Strategizing Your Splunk Implementation

3. Crafting Your Splunk Blueprint: Deployment Models Explored
4. Navigating Deployment Strategies: Choosing the Right Path
5. Deciphering Data Domiciles: Understanding Splunk's Data Storage
6. Demystifying Licensing: Unlocking the Potential Within Bounds
7. Exploring Splunk Ecosystem: Unveiling Splunk Apps
8. Practical: Illuminating Indexes
9. Practical: Splendid Splunk Apps
10. Practical: Data Ingestion Demo
11. Practical: Licensing Demystified

Section 3: Setting Up Splunk Environment

12. Crafting Cloud Comfort: Provisioning a Splunk Cloud Instance
13. Embracing Linux: Installing Splunk on Linux Systems
14. Embracing Windows: Installing Splunk on Windows Systems

Section 4: Harnessing Data Influx

15. Channeling Data: Strategies for Effective Data Ingestion
16. Configuring Inputs: Navigating the Basics
17. Forwarding Ahead: Mastering Data Forwarders
18. Hands-On: Forwarders on Linux, Unveiled
19. Hands-On: Windows Universal Forwarder Mastery
20. Hands-On: Universal Forwarder on Windows, Unveiled
21. Hands-On: Linux Forwarders, Step by Step

Section 5: Mastering Search and Analysis

22. Unveiling the Search Engine: Exploring its Inner Workings
23. Navigating Temporal Realms: Mastering Time in Searches
24. Temporal Tactics: Maximizing Time Variables in Analysis

25. Initiating the Search: Essential Techniques for Beginners
26. Fields Unleashed: Unraveling the Mysteries of Field Extractions
27. Practical: Search and Reporting App Exploration
28. Practical: Crafting Dynamic Tables and Pivots
29. Practical: Search Fundamentals and Dashboard Creation, Part 1
30. Practical: Search Fundamentals and Dashboard Creation, Part 2
31. Practical: Time Mastery in Action
32. Practical: Field Extraction in Depth
33. Beyond Basics: Unleashing the Power of Intermediate Searches, Part 1
34. Beyond Basics: Unleashing the Power of Intermediate Searches, Part 2

Section 6: Crafting Visual Insights

35. Visualizing Data Dynamics: Grasping the Fundamentals
36. Artistry in Analytics: Exploring Diverse Visualization Types
37. Constructing Data Frameworks: Unveiling the Realm of Data Models
38. Reporting Renaissance: Empowering Insights and Alerts
39. Pivot Wizardry: Harnessing the Pivot Tool for Insights
40. Practical: Crafting Dashboards with Pivot, Part 1
41. Practical: Crafting Dashboards with Pivot, Part 2
42. Practical: Exploring Dashboard Craftsmanship, Part 1
43. Practical: Exploring Dashboard Craftsmanship, Part 2
44. Practical: Building Dynamic Data Models, Part 1
45. Practical: Building Dynamic Data Models, Part 2

Section 7: Mastery of Advanced Concepts

46. Orchestrating Deployment: Managing Servers and Forwarders
47. Gatekeeping Access: Delving into User Management and Authentication, Part 1
48. Gatekeeping Access: Delving into User Management and Authentication, Part 2
49. Configuration Chronicles: Unraveling Configuration File Essentials, Part 1
50. Configuration Chronicles: Unraveling Configuration File Essentials, Part 2
51. Knowledge Repository: Harnessing the Power of Knowledge Objects
52. Lookup Labyrinth: Navigating Lookup Essentials, Part 1
53. Lookup Labyrinth: Navigating Lookup Essentials, Part 2

~ Conclusion

Section 1:
Introduction

Welcome & What You'll Learn

Welcome to the exciting world of Splunk, and congratulations on embarking on this journey of data mastery! In this book, "Mastering Splunk: A Comprehensive Guide for Beginners," I'll be your guide as we unveil the power of this remarkable technology. Splunk is an invaluable tool for anyone seeking to unlock the hidden stories within their data, and this chapter will outline what's in store.

Why Splunk?

Machine-generated data drives our digital world. Every website click, every online purchase, every sensor reading from devices – it forms a torrent of information. Splunk tames that torrent, transforming data into insights that can:

- **Troubleshoot IT problems:** Servers crash, networks slow down, why? Splunk helps you find those answers fast.
- **Monitor business performance:** Track sales trends, analyze customer behavior, and optimize operations.
- **Enhance security:** Identify threats and anomalies before they cause serious damage.

About This Book

This book is specifically designed for those new to Splunk. We'll start with the very foundations and gradually build towards advanced concepts. My goal is for you to achieve the following:

- **Understand Splunk's Core:** Explore the technology that makes Splunk work, from its architecture to data storage.
- **Install and Set Up:** Learn to provision Splunk in the cloud or install it on your local system.
- **Ingest Data:** Integrate data from diverse sources – logs, network data, application metrics, and more.
- **Search and Analyze:** Master Splunk's powerful search language and uncover patterns in your data.
- **Visualize Your Insights:** Create compelling dashboards and reports to share and act upon.
- **Master Advanced Features:** Manage users, use lookups, and delve into the details of configuration.

The Journey Ahead

This book isn't merely theoretical; practical exercises are woven throughout. You'll get hands-on, solidifying your understanding with real-world scenarios. Here's how the journey unfolds:

- **Introduction:** The basics of Splunk and laying the groundwork.
- **Strategizing Your Implementation:** Choosing deployment options, understanding data needs, and licensing.
- **Setting Up Your Environment:** Installation in the cloud or on your own systems (Linux and Windows).
- **Harnessing Data Influx:** Learning all ways to get your data flowing into Splunk.
- **Mastering Search and Analysis:** Using Splunk's search language to filter, analyze, and extract fields.
- **Crafting Visual Insights:** Charts, graphs, pivot tables, and dashboards, oh my!
- **Mastery of Advanced Concepts:** Tackling user management, lookups, configuration files, and more.

Get Ready to Become a Splunk Master

Are you ready to transform from a data novice to a Splunk master? The path isn't always easy, but with dedication, the rewards are immense. Let's buckle up and dive into Chapter 2, where we explore what Splunk truly is and how it revolutionizes the data world!

Additional Resources

- **Splunk's Official "What is Splunk?":**
  https://www.splunk.com/en_us/what-is-splunk.html
- **Splunk Tutorial (For absolute beginners):**
  https://www.splunk.com/en_us/blog/learn/splunk-tutorials.html

Unveiling Splunk: Your Gateway to Data Empowerment

Picture this: your organization is a vast, ever-growing forest of information. Every server log, network packet, customer interaction, and sensor reading is a tree within this forest. Finding insights in this dense wilderness was once an almost impossible task. But then along came Splunk – your trusty machete for the data jungle.

What Exactly *Is* Splunk?

At its core, Splunk is a powerful software platform designed to unlock the hidden value of machine-generated data. Think of it as a supercharged search engine, an adaptable analysis tool, and a visual storyteller – all rolled into one. Here's what it does:

- **Captures Data from Anywhere:** Splunk can slurp up machine data from diverse sources—servers, network devices, applications, websites, sensors… you name it. It doesn't care about the format; structured or unstructured data is all fuel for Splunk.
- **Indexes for Rapid Search:** Unlike a traditional database, Splunk creates an index of your data as it comes in. That index is like a hyper-detailed forest map, allowing for lightning-fast searches no matter the size of your data.
- **Searches and Analyzes:** Splunk has a unique search language. You type in commands, like a conversation with your data, to filter, calculate, pinpoint trends, and create statistics. No complex programming needed!
- **Visualizes Everything:** Charts, graphs, maps, tables – Splunk turns raw data into eye-catching visuals. No more boring spreadsheets; now you have actionable dashboards!

- **Alerts and Automates Actions:** Set up Splunk to watch for specific conditions. When a server goes down? An alarming pattern of login attempts? Splunk can send an alert or trigger an automated response to minimize the fallout.

Beyond IT: Splunk's Impact

While Splunk is beloved by IT professionals, its benefits extend far beyond servers and networks:

- **Business Insights:** Track sales patterns, measure marketing ROI, understand user behavior on your website – data from many departments can transform into business growth when Splunk is involved.
- **Security Superhero:** Detect anomalies, correlate events from multiple systems to uncover threats that might evade traditional security tools, and streamline incident response.
- **Industrial IoT:** Machines in factories and power plants generate tons of status and performance data. Splunk helps monitor, predict failures, and optimize operations.
- **And Much More:** Healthcare, finance, government... Every industry touched by technology can unleash new potential with Splunk.

Why Mastering Splunk Matters

In a data-drenched world, those who harness data are the ones who thrive. Splunk skills open doors:

- **Problem Solver:** Swiftly troubleshoot IT issues to minimize downtime and keep your organization running smoothly.
- **Insight Hunter:** Uncover trends, patterns, and correlations that would otherwise remain hidden – empowering better decision-making.
- **Security Vigilante:** Become the shield against cyber threats, using Splunk to detect and respond swiftly.

- **Process Optimizer:** Whether it's factory machinery or website clicks, Splunk-driven insights can streamline operations and boost efficiency.

Let the Exploration Begin!

This book is your guide to conquering the realm of Splunk. We'll cover technical foundations, explore practical use cases, and transform you into a data-wielding ninja. Buckle up!

Additional Resources

- **Splunk's "How Splunk Works:"**
  https://www.splunk.com/en_us/about-splunk/how-splunk-works.html
- **Use Cases Across Industries:**
  https://www.splunk.com/en_us/customers.html

Section 2:
Strategizing Your Splunk Implementation

Crafting Your Splunk Blueprint: Deployment Models Explored

Before diving headlong into installing Splunk, it's crucial to choose the deployment model that best aligns with your organization's needs. Think of this step as laying the architectural foundation for your Splunk journey. In this chapter, we'll examine various deployment options and guide you in making the optimal choice.

Understanding Splunk Deployment Architectures

Let's break down the key ways you can deploy Splunk and how they differ:

- **Single-Instance Deployment:** The simplest setup. Here, all Splunk's core components (indexer, search head, etc..) run on a single machine. Perfect for small-scale deployments, proof of concepts, or learning environments.
- **Distributed Deployment:** Splunk's powers scale massively by distributing its components across multiple machines. This is common for larger datasets or the need to separate functions (like indexing from searching) for performance and security advantages.

- **Splunk Cloud:** Splunk offered as a managed service in the cloud (e.g., on-demand in environments like AWS and Azure). This removes much of the setup and maintenance burden while offering flexibility.
- **Hybrid Deployments:** These mix and match elements of the models above. Perhaps you keep sensitive data on-premises in a single instance but offload less critical analysis to Splunk Cloud.

Factors to Guide Your Decision

These questions will lead you to the most suitable approach:

- **Data Volume:** How much machine-generated data are you planning to analyze daily? Larger volumes often necessitate distributed or cloud deployments for adequate processing power.
- **Scalability:** Do you anticipate significant growth in data or users? Choosing a model that accommodates scaling up (cloud or distributed) can prevent headaches later.
- **IT Resources and Expertise:** Do you have the in-house personnel to manage a self-deployed Splunk instance (think OS maintenance, updates, etc.)? Splunk Cloud lessens this operational burden.
- **Security & Compliance:** Do stringent data privacy regulations govern your industry? You might opt for a single-instance on-premises for maximum control or explore private cloud options.
- **Budget:** While Splunk Cloud offers flexible subscriptions, on-premises deployments can involve upfront hardware costs. Consider both initial and long-term expenses.

Common Scenarios & Corresponding Models

Let's look at some typical situations and the best-suited deployment models:

- **Small Business/Departmental IT:** A single-instance is a good starting point. It's easy to set up and offers centralization of data.
- **Enterprise-wide Analytics:** A distributed model provides the power to handle large data volumes and potentially separate teams needing isolated Splunk search environments.
- **Rapid Growth and Flexibility:** Splunk Cloud allows you to scale up as needs change, simplifying management.
- **Strict Regulatory Requirements:** An on-premises single instance or private cloud might be necessary for complete control over data storage.

Remember: Flexibility is Key

Splunk is adaptable! Many organizations start with a single instance for testing and evolve into distributed or hybrid models as their needs change.

Additional Resources

- **Splunk Docs: Overview of Deployment Types:** https://docs.splunk.com/Documentation/Splunk/9.2.0/Overview/AboutSplunkEnterprisedeployments
- **Choosing Between Splunk Cloud and On-Premises:** https://www.splunk.com/en_us/form/choosing_splunk.html

Next Steps

In the following chapter, we'll delve deeper into navigating deployment strategies, tailoring a step-by-step approach based on your chosen model.

Navigating Deployment Strategies: Choosing the Right Path

The last chapter introduced the various ways to architect your Splunk deployment. Now it's time to translate your blueprint into a concrete plan. This chapter will guide you through detailed considerations and steps specific to your chosen model.

Deployment Strategy for Single-Instance Splunk

If a single-instance suits your needs, here's the focus of your strategy:

1. **Hardware Sizing:**
   - **CPU & RAM:** Depends on expected data volume and search complexity. More data and intricate analysis require beefier specs. Splunk docs have hardware guidelines.
   - **Storage:** Calculate how much disk space you need based on data volume and how long you want to keep data (retention period). Factor in growth projections!
2. **Operating System:** Splunk supports popular Linux distributions (e.g., Red Hat, CentOS), Windows Server, and macOS (for testing purposes). Choose what you're most comfortable managing.
3. **Network Placement:** Where this instance resides in your network influences accessibility and data flow. Consider firewalls or other security requirements.
4. **Installation and Configuration:** Follow Splunk's well-documented installation guides for the OS you chose.

We'll cover this in-depth in Section 3 (Setting Up Splunk Environment).

Deployment Strategy for Distributed Splunk

Distributed deployments require a more granular plan:

1. **Defining Component Roles:**
   - **Indexers:** Machines that process and store the indexed data. Consider how many you need based on volume and redundancy goals.
   - **Search Heads:** Provide the user interface for searching and visualizing data. You might need multiple search heads if you have a large user base.
   - **Forwarders:** Lightweight agents deployed on machines generating data, responsible for sending that data to the indexers. We'll discuss these extensively later.
2. **Hardware Sizing (for Each Role):** Each component has distinct hardware needs. Refer to Splunk documentation for sizing recommendations.
3. **Network Design:** Distributed Splunk relies heavily on fast, reliable network connectivity between its components. Factor in bandwidth, potential bottlenecks, and security zones.
4. **Deployment Orchestration:** Tools like Ansible, Puppet, or Chef can automate the rollout of distributed configurations, streamlining large-scale setups.

Deployment Strategy for Splunk Cloud

Using Splunk Cloud simplifies many aspects:

1. **Subscription Sizing:** Splunk Cloud offers tiered pricing based on data ingestion volume. Estimate your data needs to select the appropriate plan.

2. **Region:** Choose a cloud region that makes sense for data locality (to comply with regulations) and performance (closer users mean faster responses).
3. **Cloud Provider:** Splunk Cloud is available on platforms like AWS, Google Cloud Platform, and others. Align this choice with your existing cloud infrastructure if applicable.
4. **Connectivity:** Ensure robust connectivity between your data sources and the cloud instance. Hybrid setups might involve setting up site-to-site VPN tunnels.

Important Considerations (regardless of model)

- **High Availability:** For mission-critical use cases, plan for redundancy. This might mean duplicate indexers, clusters, or failover mechanisms for search heads.
- **Security:** Implement network segmentation, access controls, and encryption best practices, especially in distributed or hybrid scenarios.
- **Testing:** Before going live, *thoroughly* test your data flow, search, and visualization functionality in a staging environment mimicking your production setup.

Additional Resources

- **Splunk Docs: Distributed Deployment Planning:** https://docs.splunk.com/Documentation/Splunk/latest/Install ation/Distributeddeploymentoverview
- **Splunk Docs: System Requirements:** https://docs.splunk.com/Documentation/Splunk/9.2.0/Install ation/Systemrequirements
- **Splunk Docs: Deployment Strategies for Splunk Cloud:** https://docs.splunk.com/Documentation/SplunkCloud/latest/ User/Deploymentstrategies

Deciphering Data Domiciles: Understanding Splunk's Data Storage

In the last chapter, we charted our deployment strategy. Now it's time to understand how Splunk meticulously organizes the influx of machine data for lightning-fast retrieval and analysis. Imagine your Splunk instance as a super-organized library, and let's explore its shelves and card catalogs.

The Essence of Indexes

At the heart of Splunk's storage lies the concept of an index. An index is *not* like your standard database index. Instead, think of it as a purpose-built repository with special optimizations for both storing and searching machine data. You can have multiple indexes to logically separate different data types (e.g., web server logs in one index, firewall logs in another).

Under the Hood of an Index

Let's break down what's inside an index:

- **Raw Data:** This is the unaltered data Splunk ingests, compressed for storage efficiency.
- **Metadata:** Splunk extracts key metadata like timestamps, source of the data, the host it came from, etc. This metadata is what fuels super-fast searches.
- **Index Files ("Buckets"):** The meat of the index. Data is split into 'buckets' organized by time ranges. This bucket structure is what allows Splunk to narrow searches to specific time windows rapidly.

Hot, Warm, and Cold Buckets

Buckets aren't static; Splunk manages data lifecycle with these stages:

- **Hot:** Freshly indexed data lands in hot buckets, ready for active searching.
- **Warm:** Over time, hot buckets roll over into warm buckets. Data here is still searchable, but with slightly less immediacy than hot data.
- **Cold:** Eventually, warm buckets become cold. This data may be moved to slower storage or even archived according to your retention policies.

Strategic Index Planning

Designing your index structure is part of your deployment strategy:

- **Naming:** Descriptive index names help organize data logically.
- **Retention Policies:** Define how long you'll keep data in each index (and overall), balancing storage costs vs. analysis needs.
- **Volume:** Larger indexes may need to be split across multiple physical disks for performance.
- **Security:** Specific indexes can have fine-grained access controls applied if the data they contain is sensitive.

Key Points to Understand

- Splunk does **NOT** alter your raw data; it's kept intact for auditing or re-indexing if needed.
- Indexes are designed for speed. Splunk's search language is optimized to leverage indexes effectively.
- Index management means striking a balance between storage costs and the length of time you need to search historical data.

Practical Considerations

- **Disk Space:** Plan storage capacities by factoring in expected data volume and retention periods.
- **Indexers in a Distributed Setup:** Indexers are the workhorses that store and process data. Your deployment plan will scale these based on data load.

Additional Resources

- **Splunk Docs: About Indexes:**
  https://docs.splunk.com/Documentation/Splunk/latest/Index er/Aboutindexes
- **Splunk Docs: How the Indexer Stores Data:**
  https://docs.splunk.com/Documentation/Splunk/latest/Index er/Howtheindexerstoresindexeddata

Looking Ahead

Knowing how Splunk stores data is key, but what about the price of admission? In the next chapter, we'll tackle the crucial topic of how Splunk licensing works.

Demystifying Licensing: Unlocking the Potential Within Bounds

Splunk is an incredibly powerful tool, and its licensing model reflects the value it provides. Understanding licensing is crucial for budgeting and ensuring you're getting the most out of your Splunk investment. In this chapter, we'll shed light on how Splunk licensing works and considerations that impact it.

Splunk's Licensing Core: Data Ingestion Volume

At its heart, Splunk licenses are primarily based on the amount of machine data you ingest daily. This is usually measured in gigabytes per day (GB/day). Let's say you have a license for 100 GB/day – that means you can send up to 100 gigabytes of log data, network data, or any other machine data into Splunk each day.

License Types

Splunk offers various license types to meet different use cases and budgets:

- **Enterprise License:** The most common type. This licenses a specific daily ingestion volume.
- **Workload Licensing:** This model centers on compute resources (e.g., CPU, memory) rather than a pure focus on ingestion volume. Best for workloads with predictable resource usage.
- **Infrastructure Licensing:** Designed for scenarios where data volumes are hard to estimate. Licensing is based on the number of monitored servers, endpoints, or network devices.

- **Free License:** Allows limited ingestion (up to 500MB/day) ideal for testing and small deployments.
- **Developer Licenses:** For development and testing environments, providing generous ingest limits with restrictions on production use.

Important Considerations

- **Exceeding Ingestion:** Sometimes data volumes spike. Splunk provides some flexibility, but consistently exceeding your limits can lead to extra costs or search functionality being paused.
- **Data Indexing vs. Search:** Licenses control ingestion volume, not how much data you can search. Data retention (how long Splunk keeps data) factors into disk storage needs, but not directly into licensing.
- **Cloud vs. On-Premises:** Splunk Cloud often utilizes subscription models (pay per month), while on-premises deployments might involve larger upfront costs.

Factors that Influence Your License Needs

- **Data Sources:** How many servers, network devices, applications, etc., will you generate data from?
- **Data Verbosity:** Some data types are more 'chatty' than others (verbose logs vs. simple metrics).
- **Compliance Requirements:** Retention periods might necessitate larger licenses if you need to store data for extended periods.

Strategic Tips

- **Start Small & Scale:** Begin with a license aligning with your immediate needs. Splunk allows you to increase the license capacity later as you grow.
- **Leverage the Free License:** Perfect for proof-of-concepts or testing Splunk in a limited capacity.

- **Negotiate:** Especially for larger deployments, don't be afraid to negotiate with Splunk for the best pricing package.
- **Evaluate Alternatives:** In some rare cases, open-source alternatives to Splunk might fit. Assess these carefully, considering total cost of ownership (support, manpower, etc.).

Additional Resources

- **Splunk Docs: Licensing Overview:** https://docs.splunk.com/Documentation/Splunk/latest/Admin/Moreaboutlicenses
- **Understanding Splunk Pricing:** https://www.splunk.com/en_us/pricing.html

Up Next

Licensing is key, but it's useless if you don't have powerful add-ons! In the next chapter, we'll explore the world of Splunk apps that extend functionality and provide turn-key solutions.

Exploring Splunk Ecosystem: Unveiling Splunk Apps

Think of Splunk as the foundation of your data analytics house, and Splunk apps as the pre-built rooms that accelerate and expand what you can do. This chapter will guide you through the world of Splunk apps, showing you how they enhance your deployment and save you from reinventing the data wheel.

What Exactly Are Splunk Apps?

- **Bundles of Functionality:** Apps are pre-packaged extensions. They include things like dashboards, visualizations, pre-written searches, configurations, custom commands, and more.
- **Focused Solutions:** Apps are often designed for specific technologies (e.g., Cisco networks, Apache web servers) or address particular use cases (IT security, troubleshooting, etc.).
- **Splunkbase: Your App Marketplace:** Splunkbase (https://splunkbase.splunk.com/) is the official repository where you can browse and download thousands of free and paid Splunk apps.

Why Splunk Apps Matter

1. **Accelerate Your Time to Value:** Why spend days building a dashboard when a robust app does the heavy lifting? Apps help you extract insights faster.
2. **Tap into Deep Expertise:** Many apps are built by vendors for their own technologies or developed by Splunk experts with rich domain knowledge.
3. **Extend Core Splunk:** Apps can add capabilities not natively in Splunk, like specialized visualizations or integrations with 3rd party systems.

4. **Community Power:** The Splunk community contributes valuable apps, fostering solutions and knowledge sharing.

Types of Splunk Apps

Let's differentiate the key app flavors:

- **Apps:** These are full-blown extensions, offering dashboards, reports, new search commands, data collection setup help, and more. Think of them as 'feature packs'.
- **Add-ons:** More technical than apps, add-ons often focus on enabling data ingestion from specific sources. They might provide modular inputs or technology-specific knowledge (e.g., parsing complex firewall logs).

App Hunting: What to Look For

- **Problem Alignment:** Does the app directly address a problem you need to solve with Splunk? Don't be distracted by shiny features you might never use.
- **Support & Maintenance:** Is the app actively maintained by the developer? Is it compatible with your Splunk version?
- **Documentation:** Well-documented apps are easier to adopt and integrate into your workflows.
- **Splunk Certification:** Splunk-certified apps undergo additional reviews, providing a measure of trust and reliability.

Strategic Use of Apps

- **Inspiration:** Even if an app isn't a perfect fit, study its design to spark ideas for your custom dashboards or searches.
- **Building Blocks:** Apps often contain reusable components you can incorporate into your own work

- **Proof of Concept Acceleration:** Apps can help quickly demonstrate Splunk's value on a specific data source or use case to stakeholders.

Additional Resources

- **Splunkbase:** https://splunkbase.splunk.com/
- **Understanding Splunk Apps & Add-ons:** https://docs.splunk.com/Documentation/Splunk/9.2.0/Admin/Whatsanapp

Next Steps

Apps are a powerful tool, but understanding your data is still essential. In the next chapter, we'll do a practical exercise illuminating how Splunk indexes work, forming the basis of all your searches and analysis!

Practical: Illuminating Indexes

In previous chapters, we discussed the theoretical aspects of Splunk Indexes. Now it's time to get under the hood and see them in action. This hands-on exercise will deepen your understanding, paving the way for effective search and analysis later on.

Objectives

- Observe how raw data gets turned into index files.
- Explore index directory structures.
- Understand the key metadata Splunk extracts during indexing.

Prerequisites

- A Splunk instance (local, cloud, or even the free version will do).
- Some sample data ingested into Splunk. If you don't have any, Splunk has tutorials with sample data you can generate.

Step 1: Locate Your Index Directories

1. Navigate to your Splunk installation. There's a default location for indexes, often something like:
   - **Linux:** /opt/splunk/var/lib/splunk
   - **Windows:** C:\Program Files\Splunk\var\lib\splunk
2. Inside, you'll find directories named after your indexes (e.g., "main", "web_logs," etc.). *Don't modify raw files in these directories manually!*

Step 2: Anatomy of an Index Directory

1. Pick an index directory to explore. Inside, you'll typically find:

- Buckets: Folders typically named with a date range (e.g., db_1672521160_1672606981_10). These are the heart of where your data lives.
- Metadata Files: Files starting with ".tsidx", ".data", these hold metadata, allowing Splunk to search blazingly fast.

Step 3: Examine a Bucket

1. Open a bucket folder. Here's what you might find:
    - rawdata: Your uncompressed, original log data (or whatever data source you have).
    - Index file (extension .tsidx): This is your primary index file, with pointers to where the terms you search for are located in the raw data.
    - Other metadata files: These aid in search optimization and management.

Step 4: (Optional): Peeking at Raw Data & Metadata

1. IMPORTANT: Be careful; modifying these files can corrupt your index. View them only for learning purposes.
2. Use a text editor to look at the 'rawdata' file. You'll see your unprocessed events.
3. Metadata files are less human-readable but can give you hints into the terms and timestamps Splunk extracts.

Key Takeaways

- *Indexes are NOT Copies of Raw Data: Splunk maintains your original data *and* builds efficient search structures around it.
- Bucketing is for Time-Based Searches: Splunk's time-focused optimizations become clear when you see how data is split.
- Metadata is the Magic: The files accompanying your raw data are what power Splunk's search speed.

Additional Resources

- **Splunk Docs: Inside Splunk Indexers (more technical):**
  https://docs.splunk.com/Documentation/Splunk/latest/Index
  cr/InsideaSplunkindexer
- **Blog Post: Understanding Splunk Indexes (Beginner Friendly):**
  https://www.splunk.com/en_us/blog/tips-and-tricks/understa
  nding-splunk-indexes.html

Coming Up Next

Indexes are powerful, but they only shine when coupled with Splunk apps. In the next practical chapter, we'll explore the world of Splunkbase and see how apps extend what you can do!

Practical: Splendid Splunk Apps

In the previous chapter, we explored how Splunk indexes your data. Now, let's boost your Splunk experience by putting Splunk apps to work. This hands-on chapter will guide you through finding, installing, and leveraging apps to save time and unlock new capabilities.

Prerequisites

- Access to a Splunk instance where you have permission to install apps.
- A basic understanding of Splunk navigation.
- Internet access to browse Splunkbase.

Step 1: Mission: Define Your App Hunt

Before diving into Splunkbase, ask yourself:

- **Problem to Solve:** What specific analysis do I want to streamline, or what data source do I need better visibility into?
- **Functionality Desired:** Do I need pre-built dashboards, new visualizations, specialized search commands, or automated data collection help?

Step 2: Exploring Splunkbase

1. **Navigate to Splunkbase:** Visit https://splunkbase.splunk.com/.
2. **Search Strategies:**
   - Use the search bar with keywords relevant to your technology (e.g., "Apache", "Cisco firewall"), problem domain ("troubleshooting", "security"), or desired visualizations ("network map").

- ○ **Utilize Filters:** Refine results by categories (apps, add-ons), support status, Splunk compatibility, and pricing.
3. **Assessing an App:**
   - ○ Screenshots and descriptions provide insight into what the app offers.
   - ○ Reviews and ratings offer community feedback.
   - ○ Documentation is crucial – a well-documented app is easier to use effectively.

Step 3: Installing an App

1. **Download:** On Splunkbase, download the app file to your computer.
2. **Splunk Web:** In your Splunk instance, go to the "Manage Apps" page (the gear icon near the top left).
3. **Upload and Install:** Click "Install app from file" and choose the downloaded file. Follow the prompts.
4. Restart?: Some apps may require restarting your Splunk instance.

Step 4: Splendid Apps in Action!

- **Find New Features:** Installed apps often add new items to your Splunk navigation sidebar. Explore these!
- **Explore Dashboards:** Apps often come loaded with pre-configured dashboards providing immediate insights.
- **Learn New Tricks:** Did the app introduce custom search commands? Experiment with them in Splunk's search bar.

Example Scenario

Let's say you're tasked with monitoring your company's website built on Apache web servers:

1. **Splunkbase Search:** "Apache"

2. **Consider a combo:** "Apache Web Server App" (dashboards and web analysis) + "Apache HTTP Server Add-on" (data collection aid).
3. **Post-Install:** Watch those dashboards populate, and if needed, configure the add-on to pull data from your Apache servers.

Additional Resources

- **Splunk Docs: Browse Apps & Add-ons:**
  https://docs.splunk.com/Splexicon:Browsing_apps_and_add-ons
- **Community Blog: Splunkbase Tips:**
  https://www.splunk.com/en_us/blog/splunkbase.html

Key Takeaways

- Think of Splunkbase as your Splunk power-up library. It can accelerate your time to value massively.
- Not every app will be a perfect fit. Be prepared to experiment.

Up Next

Apps are only as good as the data you feed them! In the next practical chapter, we'll demonstrate data ingestion processes, the lifeline of your Splunk deployment.

Practical: Data Ingestion Demo

We've learned *about* data ingestion, and apps make it easier. Now's your chance to see it happen. In this practical, we'll walk through ingesting some sample data, and focus on how your choices during this process shape how you'll later analyze that data in Splunk.

Objectives

- Experience the key steps of onboarding data into Splunk.
- Understand how source types and other settings influence usability.
- Troubleshoot common data ingestion issues.

Prerequisites

- Access to a Splunk instance (any type will do).
- Permissions to add new data inputs.
- Sample data file. Splunk has some built-in, but you can use your own log file.

Scenario: Ingesting Web Server Logs

Let's pretend you need to monitor web access logs (a common Splunk use case). We'll walk through a typical ingestion setup.

Step 1: Locate Your 'Add Data' Area

- In Splunk Web, there's usually an "Add Data" option prominently displayed on the homepage, or within a settings menu.

Step 2: Data Onboarding Wizard

Splunk guides you with these steps:

1. **Upload:** Choose the way to get your data into Splunk:
   - Upload a file from your computer.
   - Monitor an ongoing stream of data from a network port.
   - Forward data from a Universal Forwarder (covered later in the book).
2. **Source Type:** THIS IS CRUCIAL! Do you have Apache logs, IIS logs, some custom format? Choose carefully, as Splunk tries to auto-detect how to parse your data based on this.
3. **Input Settings:**
   - **Host:** A logical name for the *source* of the data (e.g., WebServer1).
   - **Index:** Select where to store this data (or create a new index).
4. **Review:** Chance to double-check your choices before finalizing.

Step 3: Searching Your New Data

- Use Splunk's search bar like this:
  `sourcetype="your_chosen_sourcetype"`
- Success? You should see your raw log events appear!
- No results? Time to troubleshoot…

Troubleshooting 101

- **Wrong file format?** Double-check the source type you chose. Splunk makes its best guess but might need help.
- **Timestamps messed up?** Splunk needs to know when things happened. Check time zone settings during input configuration.
- **Still no luck?** Splunk Docs to the rescue! Search by your source type for more specific guidance.

Key Takeaways

- ***Source Types Matter!***: Picking the right one enables field extractions (unlocking powerful analysis later).
- **Experiment:** Try ingesting the same data file with *different* source types – see how the search results change.
- **Data Doesn't Lie, Settings Might:** If your data looks wrong in Splunk, revisit your input configuration.

Additional Resources

- **Splunk Docs: Adding Data:**
  https://docs.splunk.com/Documentation/Splunk/9.2.0/Data/Getstartedwithgettingdatain

Practical: Licensing Demystified

In a previous chapter, we tackled the theory of Splunk licensing. Now it's time to roll up our sleeves and see how it translates within your Splunk instance. Our goal is to give you tools to check your current usage and make informed decisions about future capacity.

Objectives

- Learn where to monitor your Splunk license usage.
- Understand common license warnings and what to do about them.
- Practice basic license capacity calculations.

Prerequisites

- Access to a Splunk instance where you have at least read-access to the licensing settings.
- Basic understanding of how Splunk licensing is measured (data ingestion per day).

Step 1: Finding Your Licensing Dashboard

- In Splunk Web, navigate to Settings (gear icon).
- Locate the "Licensing" area. This might be its own top-level option or within a monitoring console.

Step 2: Deciphering the Dashboard

Common elements on a Splunk licensing dashboard:

- **Usage:** Shown visually (graph over time) and often in a numerical format (e.g., "7.2 GB out of 10 GB used today").
- **License Type:** Enterprise, Free, Forwarder, etc.
- **Expiration/Renewal:** Important dates!
- **Warnings:** Flashing red messages? Those mean you might be exceeding your license soon.

Step 3: Investigating Warnings

Typical Warnings you might see:

- **Search Head Licensing Violation:** Too much data is being searched across your deployment (this is separate from the core ingestion limit).
- **Volume Exceeded:** You've ingested more data than your license allows in a 24-hour period.
- **License Expiration Soon:** Time to prepare for renewal.

Important: Warnings are temporary. Consult Splunk Docs for what actions (if any) result in penalties.

Step 4: Practice Time (Simple Calculations)

1. **Data per Source Type:** In Splunk, try a search like: `index=* | stats sum(linecount) as TotalEvents by sourcetype` This helps see which data sources are most 'chatty'.
2. **Rough Daily Average:** If you know how long you've been ingesting data, you can eyeball an average daily volume.
3. **Is It Close to My Limit?** Compare your estimated average ingestion to your license capacity. Leave room for spikes!

Additional Resources

- **Splunk Docs: Monitoring Your License Usage:** https://docs.splunk.com/Splexicon:Monitoring_license_usage
- **Splunk Docs: Types of Licenses:** https://docs.splunk.com/Splexicon:License_types

Key Takeaways

- Licensing isn't meant to be scary. Splunk provides tools to monitor it.

- Proactive is Better:** Address warnings before they become problems.
- Estimating Data Growth:** Think about the future. Will new systems being monitored push you over your limits?

Final Note

Licensing is complex, especially for large deployments. If you're ever in doubt, don't hesitate to work with your Splunk account representative or consult a qualified Splunk partner.

Section 3:
Setting Up Splunk Environment

Crafting Cloud Comfort: Provisioning a Splunk Cloud Instance

Harnessing the power of Splunk doesn't always mean installing it on your own servers. Splunk Cloud offers a compelling alternative, letting you focus on analyzing data, not managing infrastructure. In this chapter, we'll guide you through setting up your first Splunk Cloud instance.

Why Splunk Cloud?

- **Reduced Setup Hassle:** Get a Splunk environment up and running in minutes, not days.
- **Scalability on Demand:** Need to handle sudden data surges? Splunk Cloud can flex to match your needs.
- **Simplified Management:** Leave much of the software updates and maintenance to Splunk.
- **Things to Consider:** Cloud options can have different pricing models and some feature limitations compared to on-premises (always check the latest details).

Prerequisites

- A decision that Splunk Cloud aligns with your organization's requirements.
- A basic understanding of cloud service concepts (but don't worry, we'll clarify anything Splunk-specific).

Step 1: Begin Your Splunk Cloud Journey

1. **Navigate:** Visit the Splunk Cloud website https://www.splunk.com/en_us/cloud.html
2. **Start a Trial:** Often the best way to get hands-on. Splunk offers free trials with a limited data ingestion rate.
3. **Or Get Serious:** If you're ready to commit, the "Buy Now" options will connect you with sales.

Step 2: Provisioning Your Instance

The process is usually guided, but expect to provide details like:

- **Region:** Choose a datacenter location close to your users or data sources for optimal performance.
- **Workload Type:** Not always present, but guides Splunk in optimizing your setup based on your use cases.
- **Initial Ingestion Volume:** Your best guess about how much data you'll send to Splunk Cloud daily. This influences pricing tiers.
- **Account Details:** Setup your Splunk Cloud login credentials.

Step 3: Welcome to Your New Splunk Home

1. **The Cloud Portal:** This is different than Splunk Web. It's where you manage cloud-specific settings (billing, users, etc.).
2. **Accessing Splunk Web:** Your instance has a unique URL. Use this to start analyzing data.

Step 4: Sending Data to the Cloud

There are several ways:

- **Forwarders:** Just like with an on-premises Splunk, forwarders can send data from your network to Splunk Cloud. Configuration needs to point them to the right address.
- **Cloud Gateway (Splunk Option):** Helps send data from cloud-based sources that might be hard to reach otherwise.
- **HTTP Event Collector (HEC):** An API way to ship data into Splunk. Great for custom scripts and integrations.

Additional Resources

- **Splunk Docs: Getting Started with Splunk Cloud:** https://docs.splunk.com/Documentation/SplunkCloud/latest/User/WelcometoSplunkCloud
- **Splunk's Cloud Pricing Page:** https://www.splunk.com/en_us/products/pricing.html#cloud

Key Takeaways

- Splunk Cloud simplifies deployment, letting you focus on getting value from your data faster.
- Understanding data flow to the cloud is crucial, especially if coming from on-prem systems
- The Splunk Cloud trial makes experimenting with the platform easy.

Next Up

Whether in the cloud or on your servers, Splunk thrives on Linux. In the next chapter, we'll tackle installing Splunk on Linux systems.

Embracing Linux: Installing Splunk on Linux Systems

Linux is in Splunk's DNA. Many large-scale deployments leverage its efficiency and flexibility. Whether you're a seasoned Linux admin or a relative beginner, this chapter will guide you through a smooth Splunk installation.

Why Splunk on Linux?

- **Performance & Stability:** Linux distros are renowned for their performance in server environments, aligning well with Splunk's resource needs.
- **Customization:** Linux grants you granular control over the installation, perfect for fine-tuning Splunk to your liking.
- **Community:** There's a wealth of Linux knowledge online to help if you encounter challenges.

Prerequisites

- A Linux system (we'll cover popular distros).
- Root (or sudo) privileges for installation.
- Basic command-line familiarity.

Step 1: Choose Your Linux Flavor

Splunk officially supports common distributions like:

- Red Hat Enterprise Linux (RHEL)
- CentOS
- Ubuntu
- Debian
- SUSE

Check Compatibility: Always reference the latest Splunk documentation for supported versions of your chosen distro.

Step 2: Downloading Splunk

1. **Visit the Splunk Download Page:**
   https://www.splunk.com/en_us/download/splunk-enterprise.html
2. **Select "Linux" and the package type:**
   - `.tgz` (a compressed archive) is common for manual installs.
   - `.rpm` and `.deb` packages work with distro-specific package managers.

Step 3: Installation

Let's use a `.tgz` example, adjusting the filename for your downloaded version.

1. **Decide Install Location:** `/opt` is traditional: `sudo mkdir /opt/splunk`
2. **Extract:** `sudo tar -xvzf splunk-9.2.0-123456build-linux-2.6-x86_64.tgz -C /opt/splunk`
3. **Ownership:** Splunk should run as a non-root user: `sudo chown -R splunk:splunk /opt/splunk` (create a 'splunk' user if needed)

Step 4: Starting Splunk

1. **Become the 'splunk' user (if you created one):** `sudo su - splunk`
2. **Navigate to Splunk's bin directory:** `cd /opt/splunk/bin`
3. **Start it up:** `./splunk start --accept-license`

     ○ The first run will prompt to create an admin user.

Step 5: Accessing Splunk Web

1. **Open a web browser** on a machine that can access your Linux server.
2. **URL:** http://<your_server_hostname>:8000
3. **Login:** Use the credentials you created during first-run.

Additional Resources

- **Splunk Docs: Install on Linux:**
  https://docs.splunk.com/Documentation/Splunk/latest/Install ation/InstallonLinux

Key Takeaways

- Linux offers various ways to get Splunk installed; pick what aligns with your comfort level.
- Pay close attention to file permissions! Splunk needs access to its own files.
- Splunk docs are your friends, especially for very specific Linux distribution quirks.

Up Next

Splunk thrives on data, which often lives out on the network. In the next chapter, we'll conquer installing Splunk on Windows, enabling it to tap into Windows-specific data sources.

Embracing Windows: Installing Splunk on Windows Systems

Windows holds a vast trove of machine data, and Splunk is the key to unlocking it. Whether you prefer a graphical installer or the power of the command line, we'll cover the essential steps to get Splunk up and running in your Windows environment.

Why Splunk on Windows?

- **Windows Expertise:** If your team is strong in Windows administration, it makes managing Splunk feel more natural.
- **Native Data Sources:** Windows logs (Event Logs, performance counters, etc.) integrate smoothly with Splunk.
- **Active Directory Integration:** Splunk can tie into your user directory for authentication and auditing.

Prerequisites

- A supported Windows version (Windows Server 2012 or newer is typical, desktops work too!)
- Local administrator rights for the installation process.
- Basic familiarity with navigating Windows systems.

Step 1: Get Your Splunk Installer

1. **Splunk Website:** Visit the download page https://www.splunk.com/en_us/download/splunk-enterprise.html
2. **Choose Windows:** You'll likely want the `.msi` installer package.

Step 2: Launching the Installer

1. **Double-click:** Run the downloaded `.msi` file.

2. **Wizard:** Follow the guided installer interface:
   - **License Agreement:** A must-read!
   - **Install Location:** The default (e.g., `C:\Program Files\Splunk`) is usually fine.
   - **Admin Credentials:** Provide an admin username and password for the initial Splunk setup.

Step 3: Alternative: Command-Line Install

For more control or automation, the `.msi` can do a silent install:

```
msiexec.exe /i
splunk-9.2.0-123456build-windows-x64-release.msi
/quiet
```

- **Adjust the filename** to match your downloaded version.
- **More Options:** Check Splunk documentation for additional command-line parameters to customize the install.

Step 4: Welcome to Splunk Web

1. **Browser Time:** Open a web browser on your Windows machine (or one that can access it).
2. **Go to:** http://<your_server_hostname>:8000
3. **Login:** Use the admin credentials you set during installation.

Additional Resources

- **Splunk Docs: Install on Windows:**
  https://docs.splunk.com/Documentation/Splunk/latest/Installation/InstallonWindows

Key Takeaways

- The Windows installer makes Splunk setup a breeze for most users.

- Command-line options are there if you need advanced deployment scenarios.
- Splunk on Windows feels familiar to those accustomed to the OS.

Up Next

Now that we have Splunk installed, the real fun begins! The next chapter will focus on strategies for getting the right data flowing into your Splunk environment.

Section 4:
Harnessing Data Influx

Channeling Data: Strategies for Effective Data Ingestion

Think of Splunk as a mighty analytics engine, and data as its fuel. This chapter focuses on strategies to get the right fuel flowing in the right way: efficiently, reliably, and at the scale you need.

Understanding Data Ingestion Methods

Splunk offers several ways to get your data onboard:

- **Uploading:** Best for one-time loads of files you have locally (e.g., historical logs).
- **Monitoring:** Splunk watches files as they're written. Great for ongoing log files.
- **Network Input:** Splunk listens on a port, letting devices send data directly (think syslog or custom apps).
- **Forwarders:** Lightweight agents (we'll cover these in detail later) that push data to Splunk.
- **Modular Inputs:** Specialized data collection, often provided by Splunk Apps.

Key Strategic Questions

1. **Data Source Types:**
   - Structured logs? (Web servers, firewalls)
   - OS metrics? (Windows performance counters)

- Proprietary app output?
- Sensor data (IoT)?

2. **Push vs. Pull:**
   - Can Splunk reach the data source to pull data?
   - Or does the source need to send (push) the data to Splunk?
3. **Data Velocity:**
   - Small, periodic log files?
   - Massive high-speed streams of real-time events?
4. **Location, Location…:**
   - In the cloud? On-premises behind firewalls? Spread across a global network?

Essential Best Practices

- **Plan for Growth:** Your data volumes WILL likely expand over time. Architect to handle the future, not just today.
- **Source Types Matter A Lot:** Choosing the right input method and configuration is crucial for Splunk to parse data correctly.
- **Network Considerations:** Firewalls, bandwidth, and the reliability of links between your data and Splunk are key.
- **Data Transformation (When Needed):** Can you cleanse or enrich data before it lands in Splunk? This can sometimes save headaches later.

Scenario: A Typical Log-Centric Setup

1. **Apache Web Servers:** Forwarders installed on web servers monitor access logs, sending them to Splunk.
2. **Network Routers:** Configured to send syslog data directly to a network port Splunk listens on.
3. **Security System:** A Splunk App has a modular input to fetch alerts from your security tool's API.

Additional Resources

- **Splunk Docs: Getting Data In:**
  https://docs.splunk.com/Documentation/Splunk/latest/Data/
  Getstartedwithgettingdatain
- **Splunkbase Apps for Specific Tech:**
  https://splunkbase.splunk.com/

Up Next

We understand the "why" behind data ingestion choices. Now, let's get hands-on! The next chapter will focus on configuring basic data inputs within Splunk.

Configuring Inputs: Navigating the Basics

In the previous chapter, we discussed the big picture of data ingestion. Now, it's time to roll up our sleeves and actually tell Splunk where to find the data and how to understand it.

Objectives

- Learn how to configure the most common input types.
- Understand the importance of source types.
- Troubleshoot basic data input issues.

Prerequisites

- Access to your Splunk instance with the ability to add data inputs.
- A sample data file or an ongoing stream of data you can tap into.

Navigating Splunk's "Add Data" Area

1. **Locate:** Within Splunk Web, there's usually a prominent "Add Data" button or a similar option in the settings.
2. **The 3-Step Process:** Splunk generally guides you through:
   - **Upload/Monitor/Network:** How is Splunk getting the data?
   - **Source Type:** What kind of data is it? (This is VERY important)
   - **Input Settings:** Optional details (host, index)

Scenario 1: Ingesting a Web Server Log File

1. **Upload:** You have an archived `access.log`. Choose the "Upload" option.

2. **Source Type:** Splunk will try to guess, but often you'll select from a list: `apache_access_common`, `iis`, `nginx`, or a generic option like `access_combined`.
3. **Input Settings:**
   - **Host:** Give this data a logical name (e.g., 'WebServer01')
   - **Index:** Choose where to store the data.

Scenario 2: Monitoring a Growing Log File

1. **Monitor:** Point Splunk at a file path (`/var/log/myapp.log`).
2. **Source Type:** Critical! Pick the most accurate match, or create a custom one later if needed.
3. **Input Settings:** Same as with uploading.

Scenario 3: Network Port

1. **Network:** Specify:
   - **Port:** 514, common for syslog
   - **Protocol:** TCP or UDP
2. **Source Type:** Use `syslog` or a specialized source type provided by a Splunk app for your device.

Key Takeaways

- *Source Type Is King!* Correct source types unlock Splunk's ability to parse and search your data meaningfully.
- *Indexing at Input Time:* Think about whether you need to segregate different data types into separate indexes for better search performance or access control.
- *Don't Fear Mistakes:* You can often adjust input settings even after data is ingested.

Troubleshooting 101

- **No Data?** Double-check file paths, network firewalls, and if the source system is actually sending data!
- **Wrong Timestamps?** Time zone settings on your Splunk instance or the data source might be misconfigured.
- **Messy Fields?** The source type might be a poor fit. Experiment!

Additional Resources

- **Splunk Docs: Common Source Types:** https://docs.splunk.com/Documentation/Splunk/latest/Data/Listofpretrainedsourcetypes
- **Splunk Docs: Add Data Wizard:** https://docs.splunk.com/Documentation/AddDataWizard/latest/UserGuide/Introduction

Up Next

Simple data inputs are great, but Splunk shines on large scale! In the next chapter, we'll introduce forwarders, your key to collecting data from vast networks of machines.

Forwarding Ahead: Mastering Data Forwarders

We've learned how to get data into Splunk when you have direct access to the source system. But what if you have hundreds, or thousands, of servers scattered across a network? That's where forwarders come to the rescue.

Forwarder Fundamentals

- **Lightweight Agents:** Forwarders are like mini-Splunk instances designed to, well, forward data. They have a minimal footprint.
- **Duties:**
    - Collect data from files, network streams, etc.
    - Pre-process the data (following your instructions).
    - Securely ship data to your main Splunk instance (indexer).
- **Types:**
    - **Universal Forwarder:** The flexible workhorse. Good for most situations.
    - **Heavy Forwarder:** More features (like parsing data mid-stream), but also a larger footprint.

Why Use Forwarders?

- **Scalability:** Manage data collection across a vast distributed environment.
- **Centralized Control:** Configure forwarders from your main Splunk instance – no more logging into each remote server.
- **Network Efficiency:** Forwarders can compress data before sending, saving bandwidth.
- **Reliability:** Forwarders can queue data locally if the connection to your Splunk indexer is temporarily interrupted.

Deployment Scenarios

1. **Log-Hungry Web Farm:** Universal forwarders on each web server tail log files and send them to Splunk for analysis.
2. **Windows Domain Management:** Forwarders deployed on all Windows systems collect security events, performance counters, etc.
3. **Network Device Monitoring:** Heavy forwarders might sit near network gear, parsing syslog streams on the fly before sending enriched data to Splunk.

Managing Forwarders

- **Deployment Server (Ideal):** A dedicated Splunk instance to push configurations to your forwarder fleet. Simplifies large-scale management.
- **Manual Configuration:** Possible, but makes updates tedious as your environment grows.

Key Concepts for Configuration

- **Outputs:** You tell the forwarder WHERE to send the data (your Splunk indexer and the network port).
- **Inputs:** Just like on a regular Splunk instance, you specify what the forwarder should monitor (files, network ports, etc.).
- **Flexibility:** Forwarders can even send data to non-Splunk systems if needed.

Additional Resources

- **Splunk Docs: About Forwarders:** https://docs.splunk.com/Documentation/Splunk/latest/Forwarding/Aboutforwarders
- **Splunk Docs: Use a Deployment Server:** https://docs.splunk.com/Documentation/Splunk/latest/Updating/Configuredeploymentclients

Up Next

Theory is great, but the real power of forwarders comes to life with hands-on practice. In the next two chapters, we'll walk through installing and configuring Universal Forwarders on both Linux and Windows.

Hands-On: Forwarders on Linux, Unveiled

Objectives

- Install a Splunk Universal Forwarder on a Linux system.
- Configure the forwarder to send data to your main Splunk indexer.
- Verify data flow in Splunk Web.

Prerequisites

- A Linux system: Popular choices like Ubuntu, CentOS, or Red Hat will do.
- Root (or sudo) privileges for installation.
- A Splunk instance (indexer) ready to receive forwarded data. You should know its IP address or hostname.

Step 1: Download the Universal Forwarder

1. **Splunk Website:** Visit the download page https://www.splunk.com/en_us/download/splunk-enterprise.html
2. **Choose:** "Linux" and the correct package type for your distro (`.deb`, `.rpm`, `.tgz`)

Step 2: Installation (Example: .tgz)

1. **Copy:** Transfer the downloaded file (e.g., `splunkforwarder-9.2.0-123456build-linux-2.6-x86_64.tgz`) to your Linux system.
2. **Extract:** `tar -xvzf splunkforwarder-9.2.0-123456build-linux-2.6-x86_64.tgz -C /opt`
3. **Ownership:** `sudo chown -R splunk:splunk /opt/splunkforwarder`

Step 3: Initial Startup

1. **Become the 'splunk' user (if you created one):** `sudo su - splunk`

2. **Start Splunk:** `/opt/splunkforwarder/bin/splunk start --accept-license`
3. **Create Admin User:** Splunk will prompt for admin credentials on first run.

Step 4: Configure Forwarding

1. **Splunk Web on your indexer:** Go to Settings -> Forwarder Management (you might need to install the Deployment Management app)
2. **Add New Target:**
   - Host: IP or hostname of your Linux forwarder
   - Port: 9997 (the default)
3. **On the Linux Forwarder:**
   - `/opt/splunkforwarder/bin/splunk add forward-server <indexer_hostname_or_IP>:9997`

Step 5: Send Some Data!

1. **Monitor a File:** `/opt/splunkforwarder/bin/splunk add monitor /var/log/messages` (replace with a log file relevant to your system)
2. **Force Upload:** `/opt/splunkforwarder/bin/splunk list forward-server` (This tells the forwarder to send data immediately).

Step 6: Victory in Splunk Web

- On your Splunk indexer, search for: `index=* sourcetype="linux_messages"` (adjust the sourcetype if needed)
- If you see events rolling in, success!

Additional Resources

- **Splunk Docs: Install Universal Forwarders:**
  https://docs.splunk.com/Documentation/Forwarder/latest/Forwarder/Installanixuniversalforwarder
- **Splunk Docs: Forwarder Management:**
  https://docs.splunk.com/Documentation/Splunk/latest/Forwarding/Manageyourforwarders

Key Takeaways

- Linux install options vary slightly based on your distribution.
- Centralized forwarder management from your Splunk indexer makes life easier!

Up Next

Next, we'll conquer installing and configuring the Universal Forwarder on Windows, expanding Splunk's reach into the heart of Microsoft environments.

Hands-On: Windows Universal Forwarder Mastery

Objectives

- Install the Splunk Universal Forwarder on Windows.
- Configure the forwarder to send Windows Events to your Splunk indexer.
- Verify successful data forwarding.

Prerequisites

- A Windows system (desktop or server versions are fine).
- Administrator privileges for installation.
- Your Splunk indexer ready to receive data (IP address or hostname).

Step 1: Get the Installer

1. **Splunk Website:** Download page
   https://www.splunk.com/en_us/download/splunk-enterprise.html
2. **Select:** Windows, and the `.msi` installer.

Step 2: Installation Wizard

1. **Run the .msi:** Double-click to launch.
2. **License Agreement:** A must-read!
3. **Install Location:** The default (e.g., `C:\Program Files\SplunkUniversalForwarder`) is usually fine.
4. **Credentials:** Provide an admin username and password for Splunk to use.

Step 3: Configure Forwarding Destination

1. **Splunk Web on Your Indexer:** Go to Settings -> Forwarder Management
2. **Add New Target:**
   - **Host:** IP address or hostname of your Windows system with the forwarder.
   - **Port:** 9997 (the default)
3. **On the Windows forwarder (open a command prompt as Administrator):**
   - `cd C:\Program Files\SplunkUniversalForwarder\bin`

- ○ `.\splunk add forward-server <indexer_hostname_or_IP>:9997`

Step 4: Windows Event Fun

1. **Monitor Windows Event Logs:**
   - ○ `.\splunk add monitor "C:\Windows\System32\winevt\logs\Security.evtx"` (Collects security events)
2. **Force Upload:** `.\splunk list forward-server`

Step 5: Search Success in Splunk Web

- On your Splunk indexer, search for: `index=* sourcetype=WinEventLog:Security`
- If you see events, congrats! Your Windows insights are flowing.

Additional Resources

- **Splunk Docs: Install Universal Forwarders on Windows:** https://docs.splunk.com/Documentation/Forwarder/latest/Forwarder/InstallaWindowsuniversalforwarder
- **Splunk Docs: Monitor Windows Event Logs:** https://docs.splunk.com/Documentation/Splunk/latest/Data/MonitorWindowseventlogdata

Key Takeaways

- The Windows installer makes setup an admin-friendly breeze.
- Windows Event Logs are a treasure trove of system and security data – Splunk helps unlock it.

Up Next

Sometimes, simple forwarding isn't enough. In the next chapter, we'll look at how to configure a Universal Forwarder on Windows to handle more complex data collection scenarios.

Hands-On: Universal Forwarder on Windows, Unveiled

Objectives

- Monitor custom application log files on Windows.
- Filter data before it's sent to Splunk.
- Transform data on the forwarder to improve how it's analyzed by Splunk.

Prerequisites

- A Windows Universal Forwarder installed as covered in the previous chapter.
- Administrative access to the Windows system.
- A custom application that writes its own log files (for our example).

Scenario: Parsing a Troublesome Application Log

Your team built an in-house application. It's great, but its logs are messy. You need to ship them to Splunk, clean them up, and make them easy to search.

Step 1: Locate the Log File

Let's say our application logs to: `C:\Program Files\MyApp\logs\myapp.log`

Step 2: Configure the Forwarder (`inputs.conf`)

1. **Edit:** Navigate to `C:\Program Files\SplunkUniversalForwarder\etc\system\local` and open `inputs.conf` in a text editor.

Add a Stanza:
[monitor://C:\Program Files\MyApp\logs\myapp.log]
index = myapp
sourcetype = myapp_log

2.

Step 3: Data Transformation (`props.conf`)

The log is ugly! Each line is like: `11/25/2023 15:20:59 [ERROR] Widget Creation Failed - database timeout`

1. **Edit:** In the same directory as `inputs.conf`, open `props.conf`.

Add a Stanza:
[myapp_log]
TIME_PREFIX =^\d{2}/\d{2}/\d{4} \d{2}:\d{2}:\d{2}
TIME_FORMAT = %m/%d/%Y %H:%M:%S
MAX_TIMESTAMP_LOOKAHEAD = 20

2.
   ○ This tells Splunk how to extract the correct timestamp.

Step 4: Filtering (Optional but Powerful, `transforms.conf`)

Let's drop those noisy "INFO" level lines.

1. **Edit:** Open `transforms.conf`.

Add Stanza + Regex:
[myapp_filter]
REGEX = \[INFO\]
DEST_KEY = queue
FORMAT = nullQueue

2.
   ○ Events with "[INFO]" get dropped entirely.

Step 5: Restart the Forwarder

- **Command Prompt (as Administrator):**
  - ○ `net stop SplunkForwarder`
  - ○ `net start SplunkForwarder`

Step 6: Search in Splunk Web

- Use a search like: `index=myapp sourcetype=myapp_log ERROR`
- Your logs should be nicely formatted, with 'ERROR' events easier to find.

Additional Resources

- **Splunk Docs: Configure Forwarders:** https://docs.splunk.com/Documentation/Forwarder/latest/Forwarder/Configuretheuniversalforwarder

Key Takeaways

- Windows applications often have custom log formats. Splunk forwarders can tame them.
- Filtering data at the source saves bandwidth and indexer load.
- A bit of configuration goes a long way in making your logs Splunk-friendly.

Hands-On: Linux Forwarders, Step by Step

Objectives

- Monitor custom application logs on Linux.
- Send data from Linux forwarders via intermediate Heavy Forwarders for additional processing.
- Troubleshoot common forwarding issues on Linux.

Prerequisites

- A Linux Universal Forwarder installed, as done in a previous chapter.

- Root (or sudo) privileges for configuration.
- A custom application generating its own log files (for our example).
- A Splunk Heavy Forwarder (optional, but useful for the intermediate forwarding scenario).

Scenario: Wrangling Application Logs (Basic)

Your development team has a Linux application with logs in `/var/log/myapp/`. You need these in Splunk for troubleshooting.

Step 1: Configure Basic Monitoring (`inputs.conf`)

1. **Edit:** Navigate to `/opt/splunkforwarder/etc/system/local/` and open `inputs.conf`

Add a Stanza:
[monitor:///var/log/myapp/*.log]

index = myapp

sourcetype=linux_myapp

2.

Step 2: Restart the Forwarder

- `/opt/splunkforwarder/bin/splunk restart`

Step 3: Forward to Your Indexer

1. **Edit:** Open `outputs.conf` (same location as `inputs.conf`)

Add a Stanza:
[tcpout]

defaultGroup=indexer_group

[tcpout:indexer_group]

server=<your_indexer_hostname_or_IP>:9997

   2.

Step 4: Check Splunk Web

- Search: `index=myapp sourcetype=linux_myapp`

Scenario 2: Tiered Forwarding (with a Heavy Forwarder)

On the Heavy Forwarder (inputs.conf):
[splunktcp://9997]

   1.
      ○ This tells it to listen for data from other forwarders.
   2. **On the Universal Forwarder (outputs.conf):** Change the `server` line to point to your Heavy Forwarder.
   3. **Heavy Forwarder (outputs.conf):** Forward to your indexer as usual.

Troubleshooting Tips

- **Permissions:** Make sure the 'splunk' user can read the log files.
- **Firewalls:** Check `iptables` or similar on Linux; ensure ports 9997 (and others if using intermediate forwarders) are open.

- **Forwarder Logs:** In
  `/opt/splunkforwarder/var/log/splunk/splunkd.`
  `log`, look for errors.

Additional Resources

- **Splunk Docs: Configure Forwarding with Heavy Forwarders:**
  https://docs.splunk.com/Documentation/Forwarder/latest/Forwarder/Configuretheuniversalforwarder
- **Splunk Docs: Troubleshooting Forwarding:**
  https://docs.splunk.com/Documentation/Forwarder/latest/Forwarder/Troubleshoottheuniversalforwarder

Key Takeaways

- Linux log locations can vary – adjust paths for your application.
- Heavy Forwarders are great for pre-processing data in large deployments or reducing load on your main indexer.
- Don't be afraid of forwarder logs during troubleshooting!

You've mastered Universal Forwarder configuration on both Windows and Linux. This will significantly enhance your ability to gain insights from the vast amounts of data generated throughout your IT landscape.

Section 5:

Mastering Search and Analysis

Unveiling the Search Engine: Exploring its Inner Workings

Understanding the Search Pipeline

The moment you hit 'Enter' on a Splunk search, a multi-stage process kicks off:

1. **Parsing:** Splunk breaks down your search into terms (keywords), commands (like `sort`, `stats`), functions, and clauses.
2. **Search Job Creation:** A search job is born, managing everything about this particular search.
3. **Dispatch:** The job is sent to indexers (or in large setups, search heads distribute the workload).
4. **Index Searching:** Indexers, where the raw data lives, apply the search terms and commands. Events that *don't* match are discarded early.
5. **Results and Post-Processing:** Matching events zip back, potentially get further transformed (calculations, sorting), and then are presented to you.

Key Concepts for Optimization

- **Search Modes:** Splunk has 'Fast', 'Verbose', and 'Smart' modes. These offer a trade-off between speed and how much detail is displayed alongside your results. Start in 'Smart' mode for most use cases.
- **Time Ranges Matter:** The broader the time range, the harder Splunk works. Be specific whenever possible.
- **Fields are Your Friends:** If you only care about certain fields, tell Splunk early in the search (e.g., `sourcetype=access_log | fields ip_address status_code`). This speeds things up.
- **Order (Sometimes) Matters:** Commands that filter out events early (like `search error`) are more efficient when placed at the beginning of your search.

Example: Dissecting a Search

Let's analyze:

sourcetype=linux_syslog failed password | stats count by user | sort -count

- `sourcetype=linux_syslog`: Zooms in on a specific data type.
- `failed password`: Filters for events containing these words.
- `stats count by user`: Calculates how many failed logins per user.
- `sort - count`: Sorts in descending order of failed login attempts.

Tips for the Search Journey

- **Start Simple, Iterate:** Build searches step-by-step, adding complexity as needed.
- **Errors Are Informative:** Splunk will try to suggest fixes when a search fails. Pay attention!

- **The Search Job Inspector:** In Splunk Web, access this via the search job menu. It provides a deeper view into how Splunk executed your search.

Additional Resources

- **Splunk Docs: How Splunk Search Works:** https://docs.splunk.com/Documentation/Splunk/latest/Search/Howsearchworks
- **Splunk Docs: Search Job Inspector:** https://docs.splunk.com/Documentation/Splunk/latest/Search/Searchjobinspector

Key Takeaways

- Knowing how Splunk thinks under the hood helps you craft searches that perform well, especially at scale.
- Splunk search has nuances. Experimentation and referring to the documentation are your allies!

Up Next

Understanding how Splunk searches is powerful. But, searches are built on time! In the next chapter, we'll delve into how to master time-based searches for pinpointing the crucial data hidden within your timelines.

Navigating Temporal Realms: Mastering Time in Searches

Why Time Matters in Splunk

- **Timestamps are Everywhere:** Nearly all machine data has timestamps. They tell you *when* things happened.
- **Problem Isolation:** Did errors spike at 2:15 AM? Time-based searches will pinpoint the moment issues arose.
- **Trend Spotting:** Is performance degrading over weeks? Was there a sudden traffic surge yesterday? Visualizing data over time reveals these patterns.

The Anatomy of a Splunk Timestamp

- **Default Extraction:** Splunk usually figures out timestamps automatically during data input.
- **Hidden Fields:** Splunk stores timestamps in a special field called `_time`. It might not be displayed by default, but it's always working behind the scenes.

Specifying Time Ranges

1. **Presets:** "Last 24 hours", "Previous Month," and more. These are great for quick searches.
2. **Earliest and Latest:**
   - Examples: `earliest=-7d` (7 days ago), `latest=now` (up to this very second), `earliest=-15m` (last 15 minutes)
3. **Custom Date/Time:**
   - Example: `earliest=06/17/2023:09:00:00 latest=06/17/2023:14:30:00`

- Refer to Splunk docs for the supported date/time string formats.

Time Zones: Friend or Foe?

- **Beware:** Systems log in their *local* time zones. Is your data from machines in different time zones?
- **Splunk to the Rescue:** Your user profile in Splunk has a time zone setting. Splunk tries to display timestamps in a way that makes sense to *you*.
- **Advanced Override:** Commands exist to force time zone conversions within searches when needed.

Example: Finding a Spike

sourcetype=web_access | timechart count by status_code

- `timechart` is a powerful command for visualizing trends over time. Here, it shows access attempts grouped by HTTP status code.

Additional Resources

- **Splunk Docs: Time Modifiers in Searches:** https://docs.splunk.com/Documentation/Splunk/latest/SearchReference/SearchTimeModifiers
- **Splunk Docs: Specify Time Zone in Searches:** https://docs.splunk.com/Documentation/Splunk/latest/Search/SpecifyTimeZoneinSearches

Key Takeaways

- Mastering time ranges is fundamental to extracting meaningful answers from your data.
- Pay attention to time zones to avoid misinterpreting results.

Temporal Tactics: Maximizing Time Variables in Analysis

Snapping Time to Intervals

Events don't always happen at the perfect minute or hour. Here's how to group them into buckets:

- **The snap Argument:** Add snap to the `timechart` command or others that aggregate over time.
- **Examples:**
  - `timechart span=15m count` (15-minute buckets)
  - `timechart span=1d count` (daily buckets)

Time Calculations

- **Relative Time is Your Friend:** Want to see data from the same hour yesterday? Combine `earliest`, `latest`, and math!
  - Example: `earliest=-1d@h latest=@h`
- **Duration Magic:** Find events longer than 5 minutes? Use the `duration` field: `duration>300`

Time Magic Functions

Go beyond the basics with functions that modify time:

- **`strftime()`** Extract portions of timestamps for cleaner displays. Example: `strftime(_time, "%Y-%m-%d")`
- **`now()`** Current time, useful for comparisons.
- **`relative_time()`:** Express time relative to now. Example: `relative_time(now(), "-1d")` (yesterday)

Illustrative Scenario: User Login Patterns

```
sourcetype=authentication | timechart span=1h count by user
  WHERE earliest=-7d@d latest=@d
| eval HourOfDay=strftime(_time, "%H") | timechart count by HourOfDay
```

1. We pull a week's worth of login events.
2. Get hourly login counts per user.
3. Extract the "HourOfDay" for more granular visualization.
4. Plot overall logins per hour for the past week.

Macro Magic (Advanced)

Macros are like reusable search snippets with parameters. They can power complex time-based dashboards.

1. **Example Macro (in Splunk config):**

```
[hourly_stats_macro(30)]
definition = earliest=-$duration$h@h latest=-0h@h <Rest of your
search>
```

2. **Use It:** `hourly_stats_macro(30)`
   `sourcetype=web_access ...` (stats for the past 30 hours)

Additional Resources

- **Splunk Docs: eval Time Functions:**
  https://docs.splunk.com/Documentation/Splunk/latest/SearchReference/Eval
- **Splunk Docs: Macros:**
  https://docs.splunk.com/Documentation/Splunk/latest/Knowledge/Searchmacros

Key Takeaways

- Splunk allows for flexible ways to slice and dice time-series data.

- Calculations and functions help compare specific time periods for trend and anomaly detection.
- For complex, reusable time-based logic, consider the power of macros.

Initiating the Search: Essential Techniques for Beginners

The Search Bar: Your Splunk Compass

The Splunk Search bar is where your exploration begins. Here's the basic anatomy of a search:

search terms | command1 | command2 ...

- **Search Terms:** Keywords, phrases (in quotes), field=value pairs to narrow down the events you care about.
- **Vertical Pipe (|):** The pipeline character that passes the output of one command as input to the next.
- **Commands:** Powerful verbs that transform your data (e.g., `stats`, `top`, `search`, `eval`).

Essential Search Techniques

1. **Keywords: KISS It!** Start with simple words relevant to your question (e.g., "error", "failed", the name of an application).
2. **Filtering with Fields:**
   - Examples: `sourcetype=access_log status=500`
3. **Boolean Operators:**
   - AND (implicit if you have multiple terms)
   - OR
   - NOT
4. **Wildcards (*)** For fuzzy matching (e.g., `error code = 50*` to catch various 500-level errors)

Example: Troubleshooting a Web App

```
sourcetype=nginx "GET /api/*" status>=500 | top user_ip
```

- Limits to NGINX logs for the API section with errors.
- Calculates the top IP addresses making bad requests.

Pro Tips

- **Autocomplete is Your Friend:** Splunk suggests fields, commands, and values as you type!
- **Learn a Few Key Commands:** `stats`, `top`, `rare`, `timechart` form a powerful initial toolkit.
- **Search Modes:** Start in 'Smart Mode' for most explorations. Verbose Mode is helpful if you need to see everything Splunk is doing under the hood.

Additional Resources

- **Splunk Docs: Search Tutorial:** https://docs.splunk.com/Documentation/Splunk/latest/SearchTutorial/WelcometotheSearchTutorial
- **Splunk Docs: Search Language Reference:** https://docs.splunk.com/Documentation/Splunk/latest/SearchReference/WhatsInThisManual

Key Takeaways

- Begin with simple searches and add complexity as you get comfortable with the results.
- Boolean operators (AND, OR, NOT) help you fine-tune your focus.
- A few well-understood commands are better than trying to memorize them all.

Fields Unleashed: Unraveling the Mysteries of Field Extractions

Why Fields Matter

- **Machine Data is Messy:** Logs, events, and other data sources rarely arrive in a perfectly organized format. Fields impose structure on this chaos, making it easier to work with.
- **Search Power:** Think of fields as the labels on data elements. Need to isolate events where a transaction amount exceeds a threshold, or a username contains an invalid character? Fields allow for that surgical precision.
- **Stats and Visuals:** The real insights emerge when you can aggregate and visualize data based on these fields. What are the average response times grouped by geographical region? Which product categories generate the most support tickets? These questions are easily answered when you've extracted the relevant fields.

Splunk's Field Extraction Arsenal

1. **Automatic:** Splunk works tirelessly to automatically identify common fields like IP addresses, timestamps, hostnames, and more. You'll often see these in Splunk Web's 'Interesting Fields' sidebar during your searches.
2. **Extraction Time vs. Search Time:** Choosing the right time for extraction is important:
    - **Extraction Time:** For predictable data sources, this is the most efficient approach. Fields are permanently created when data is ingested. Look

into configuration files (`props.conf`, `transforms.conf`) to define extraction rules.

- ○ **Search Time:** Ideal for ad-hoc analysis or data sources that lack consistent structure. Commands like `rex` empower you to define extractions on the fly within a search.

Scenario: Those Pesky Apache Logs

Classic Apache logs often look like this: `123.45.67.89 - - [27/Oct/2020:09:29:12 -0700] "GET /api/user HTTP/1.1" 200 5426`

Extracting fields like `client_ip`, `timestamp`, `method`, `http_status` would vastly improve our ability to analyze these logs.

Ways to Extract Fields

1. **Configuration Files:** The ideal method for consistent data sources. Think strategically about source types and use `props.conf` and `transforms.conf` to define how Splunk should dissect your data for permanent field creation.
2. **Search Time:** The `rex` command, armed with regular expressions, is your best friend for flexible extractions within a search. This is great for one-off situations or data whose format shifts frequently.
3. **Field Extraction GUI:** Splunk Web offers a visual interface that makes it easy to experiment with field extractions. Use this to quickly test regular expressions or extract fields from sample event.

Example: `rex` in Action

```
sourcetype=apache_access | rex field=_raw "GET (?<http_path>\S+)" |
stats count by http_path
```

- `rex` command: Uses a regular expression to grab the HTTP path
- `stats count by http_path`: Shows which API endpoints are hit most frequently

Additional Resources

- **Splunk Docs: Extract Fields from Events:**
  https://docs.splunk.com/Documentation/Splunk/latest/Data/Aboutdefaultfieldsandautomaticfieldextraction
- **Splunk Docs: Regular Expressions in the `rex` command:**
  https://docs.splunk.com/Documentation/Splunk/latest/SearchReference/Rex

Key Takeaways

- Mastering field extractions transforms your searches from keyword hunting to precision targeting.
- Start with Splunk's automatic extractions, then customize for your specific data sources using `props.conf` and `rex`.
- Regular expressions are a powerful tool, and a little knowledge goes a long way! Numerous resources are available online to help you learn.

Practical: Search and Reporting App Exploration

Objectives

- Understand what Splunk Apps are and why they're important.
- Learn how to browse and install apps from Splunkbase.
- Explore key apps relevant to search and reporting use cases.

Splunk Apps: Enhancing Your Analytics

- **Pre-Built Solutions:** Apps package up dashboards, reports, field extractions, custom visualizations, new commands, and more. They often solve common problems or are tailored for specific technologies.
- **Splunkbase:** The official app marketplace https://splunkbase.splunk.com/. A vast collection of free and paid apps. Think of it like an app store for Splunk!
- **Not Just for Experts:** Even with limited Splunk development experience, apps can unlock valuable functionality with minimal setup.

Finding the Gems on Splunkbase

1. **Access:** Visit https://splunkbase.splunk.com/ in your web browser.
2. **Search:** Use the search bar to find apps relevant to your tech stack (vendor names, technologies like "Cisco", "AWS") or problem domains ("security", "performance").
3. **Filters:** Refine by categories (e.g., "Utilities", "Visualizations"), support levels, Splunk version compatibility, and more.

4. **App Details:** Each app has a description page. Pay
   attention to:
   - ○ Screenshots and documentation
   - ○ Support offered
   - ○ Reviews from other users

Installation Made Easy

1. **In Splunk Web:** Go to "Manage Apps" -> "Browse More
   Apps." This connects directly with Splunkbase.
2. **Download and Upload:** If necessary, you can download
   the app from Splunkbase as a file and then upload it to your
   Splunk instance via "Install app from file" in the app
   management interface.

Must-Have Apps for Search and Reporting

*These recommendations provide a starting point; your perfect app
combo will depend on your specific data*

- **Sideview Utils:** Adds powerful search commands, form
  enhancements, and custom visualizations. A true
  powerhouse Swiss army knife for the searching enthusiast.
- **Lookup File Editor:** Easily manage Lookup tables (more
  on those later!) through a user-friendly interface rather than
  only through configuration files.
- **Report Builder:** If the basic reporting tools aren't flexible
  enough, this app expands your ability to craft custom
  reports.
- **Visualization Apps:** Explore apps tailored to specific chart
  types (network topology maps, geographic maps, etc.)

Example: Enhancing Apache Monitoring

1. **Search:** On Splunkbase, search for "Apache".
2. **Consider:** The "Splunk App for Apache" or the "Splunk App
   for Web Analytics" depending on your focus.

3. **Install:** Follow the in-app instructions and documentation.
4. **Benefits:** You might gain pre-built dashboards, tailored field extractions for deeper Apache logs analysis, and more!

Additional Resources

- **Splunk Docs: Browse Apps:**
  https://docs.splunk.com/Documentation/Splunk/latest/Advan cedDev/CLIadmincommands#browse

Key Takeaways

- Splunkbase is a fantastic resource to save time and supercharge your Splunk skills.
- Always read documentation and check compatibility before installing apps.
- Don't be afraid to experiment! Most apps are easily uninstalled if they don't fit your needs.

Up Next

Apps often provide reports and dashboards that help you glean insights from your data. In the next chapter, we'll move beyond simple tables and cover the 'Pivot' feature – a powerful tool within Splunk for dynamically slicing, dicing, and reporting on your data.

Practical: Crafting Dynamic Tables and Pivots

Objectives

- Understand when to use tables vs. pivot reports.
- Learn to wield the `pivot` command for data restructuring.
- Build a basic pivot-driven dashboard panel.

Tables: The Familiar Format

- **Row-Based:** Each event usually gets a row, great for detailed inspection.
- **Limitations:** It can be hard to spot trends or compare multiple dimensions at once in large tables.

Enter the Pivot

- **Matrix on Steroids:** Pivots let you reshape data, putting selected fields as rows, columns, and aggregated values.
- **Why It's Awesome:**
  - See trends across multiple dimensions quickly.
  - Compare groups, like response times per URL path.
  - Calculate sums, counts, averages, etc. within pivots.

Scenario: Website Performance Troubleshooting

Our Apache access logs have these fields: `http_method`, `uri_path`, `response_time` (in seconds). We want to:

- See if certain website sections (`uri_path`) are consistently slower than others.
- Track this by HTTP method (GET, POST, etc.)

The Search

```
sourcetype=apache_access
| pivot http_method uri_path avg(response_time) AS "Avg Response"
```

Breaking It Down

1. **Base Search:** Just grabs the data we care about.
2. **pivot Command:** The magic!
   - http_method: This field becomes the columns.
   - uri_path: This field becomes the rows.
   - avg(response_time) ...: Calculates average response time and gives it a nice label.

Pivot in a Dashboard

1. **Create New Dashboard:** Give it a title (e.g., "Website Performance")
2. **Add a Panel:** Choose "Pivot" as the visualization.
3. **Paste the Search:** The same search works!
4. **Tweaks:**
   - Consider converting response time to milliseconds for better readability in dashboard cells.
   - Use Splunk's formatting features to improve presentation (e.g. heatmaps)

Additional Resources

- **Splunk Docs: The pivot Command:** https://docs.splunk.com/Documentation/Splunk/latest/SearchReference/Pivot
- **Splunk Docs: Dashboard Examples (many use Pivot):** https://docs.splunk.com/Documentation/Splunk/latest/Viz/PanelreferenceforSimplifiedXML

Key Takeaways

- Pivot is your best friend when you need a multi-dimensional view of your data.

- Don't neglect the basics: a well-structured initial search makes pivoting easier.
- Start with simple pivots, then add complexity. The pivot interface in dashboards offers a lot of options!

Up Next

Now that you can wield tables and pivots, it's time to combine these reporting techniques to build compelling dashboards. In the next chapter, we'll dive into the basics of dashboard creation!

Practical: Search Fundamentals and Dashboard Creation, Part 1

Objectives

- Understand dashboard building blocks.
- Create a simple dashboard with various visualizations.
- Learn to save and manage dashboards.

Dashboards: Your Data Insights Hub

- **Visual:** Dashboards go beyond text searches, making data easier to understand at a glance.
- **Shareable:** Great for presenting insights to teams and stakeholders who may not be Splunk search ninjas.
- **Panels:** Dashboards are made of individual panels, each holding a search result, often in the form of a visualization.

Step 1: A New Dashboard

1. **In Splunk Web:** Navigate to the Dashboards tab.
2. **Create New Dashboard:**
   - **Title:** Give it a descriptive name (e.g., "Network Errors Overview")
   - **Classic Dashboards** are recommended for beginners. We'll focus on those for now.

Step 2: Our First Panel

1. **Add a Panel Button:** Click this in your empty dashboard.
2. **New (from Search):** For most panels, we start with a Splunk search.
3. **Enter a Search:**
   ```
   sourcetype=cisco:syslog error | stats count
   by error_message
   ```

- This assumes you have network device logs.
4. **Visualization:** Start basic: choose "Pie Chart".
5. **Panel Title:** Something like "Top Error Types"
6. **Save:** Click the "Save" button at the top of the whole dashboard to preserve your work.

Step 3: Adding Variety

1. **Repeat the 'Add Panel' Process:** Experiment with searches like:
   - **Line Chart:** `sourcetype=access_log | timechart count by uri_path` (Web traffic trends over time)
   - **Single Value:** `sourcetype=linux_metrics used_memory_percent | top used_memory_percent` (Server with the highest memory usage)
   - **Table:** `sourcetype=linux_metrics top host, cpu_pct` (CPU usage per host)
2. **Arrangement:** Drag and drop panels to rearrange them to your liking.

Step 4: Dashboard Enhancements

- **Time Picker:** In the dashboard's top right corner, adjust the time range to match what your panels are visualizing. Data might not make sense if some panels show the last hour, and others the last week!
- **Explore Splunk Docs:** Check out the Dashboard Examples page for inspiration and panel configuration tips

Additional Resources

- **Splunk Docs: Building Dashboards in Classic Mode:** https://docs.splunk.com/Documentation/Splunk/latest/Viz/IntroToDashboards

- **Splunk Docs: Dashboard Examples:**
  https://docs.splunk.com/Documentation/Splunk/latest/Viz/PanelreferenceforSimplifiedXML

Key Takeaways

- Start simple! Even a few basic panels can provide valuable insights.
- Dashboard creation is iterative. Refine your layout and searches as you gain ideas and feedback.
- Don't be afraid of the vast array of visualization options – a few well-chosen ones go a long way.

Up Next

Dashboards become truly powerful when we customize searches to filter data based on user input. In the next chapter, we'll learn techniques to make our dashboards more interactive!

Practical: Search Fundamentals and Dashboard Creation, Part 2

Objectives

- Introduce dashboard input elements (dropdowns, text boxes).
- Use tokens to power dynamic searches.
- Improve dashboard aesthetics.

Scenario: User-Driven Error Analysis

Our Network Error Overview dashboard needs flexibility. What if we want to focus on errors from a specific network device, or a particular error type, without editing individual searches?

Step 1: Adding a Dropdown

1. **Edit Your Dashboard:** Click the "Edit" button on your existing dashboard.
2. **Edit a Panel:** Click the edit icon (a pencil) on a panel. Choose "Edit Inline Search" for now (we'll touch on "Edit Source" later).
3. **Add a Dropdown:**
   - Before your base search, add a line like this: `<input type="dropdown" token="error_type"></input>`
4. **Populate the Dropdown:**
   - Add a search below your main one:

```
sourcetype=cisco:syslog error
| dedup error_message
| fields error_message
```

○ Set this search to create the dropdown. Give it a "Search Label" like "Filter by Error Type".

Step 2: Tokens to the Rescue!

- **What Are Tokens?** Think of them as variables in your dashboard. The 'dropdown' input we created sets a token named `error_type`
- **Modify Your Main Search:**

sourcetype=cisco:syslog error
| search error_message=$error_type$
| stats count by error_message

- **Notice:** `$error_type$`. When the user picks an error from the dropdown, this part of the search updates.

Step 3: Repeat for Other Inputs

- Add dropdowns for device names, time ranges, etc. Each one needs a unique token name!
- **Pro Tip:** You can use text input boxes (`<input type="text"...>`), radio buttons, and more. Check the Splunk Docs for dashboard element options.

Step 4: Dashboard Polish

1. **Titles and Placement:** Make sure input elements have clear labels near them. Group related elements together.
2. **Colors and Fonts:** Under Dashboard settings, experiment with basic presentation improvements.
3. **"Edit Source" Mode:** For complex formatting, Splunk Classic dashboards have a raw XML editing mode.

Additional Resources

- **Splunk Docs: Use Input Elements on Dashboards:**
  https://docs.splunk.com/Documentation/Splunk/latest/Viz/tokens
- **Splunk Docs: Edit Dashboard Source (XML):**
  https://docs.splunk.com/Documentation/Splunk/latest/Viz/PanelreferenceforSimplifiedXML#Use_the_XML_source_editor_to_edit_a_dashboard

Key Takeaways

- Interactivity is key for dashboards targeted at non-Splunk experts.
- A few well-placed input elements can make the difference between a static report and a dynamic analysis tool.
- Don't neglect the aesthetics! A polished dashboard is easier to use and interpret.

Practical: Time Mastery in Action

Objectives

- Analyze trends with timecharts across different scales.
- Compare the same time period on different days.
- Use time functions to pinpoint issues within large datasets.

Scenario 1: Website Traffic - Is It a Daily Pattern?

- **Problem:** Web traffic spikes at certain hours, but is it consistent, or are 'bad' days different?
- **Search:**

```
sourcetype=access_log
| timechart span=1h count by status_code
```

- **Tweak:** Add | `eval` `day_of_week=strftime(_time,"%A")` to see trends grouped by the day of the week.

Scenario 2: Shifting Baselines

- **Problem:** Errors seem higher, but is it gradual, or did something suddenly break?
- **Search:**

```
sourcetype=cisco:syslog error
| timechart count AS today
| appendpipe [search sourcetype=cisco:syslog error
earliest=-7d@d latest=-6d@d
| timechart count AS "Same Day Last Week"]
```

      ○ Uses advanced features (subsearches, appendpipe) to overlay last week's data on the current week.

Scenario 3: When Did It Break?

- **Problem:** A batch job usually finishes in 20 minutes. Logs show it's failing, but when did this start?
- **Searches:**
  1. `sourcetype=batch_job status=failed | timechart count` (General timeframe)
  2. ```
     | eval runtime=duration
      | where runtime > 1200
      | table _time, runtime
      ``` (Zoom in on failures, find the
     first long runtime)
     ```

Additional Tips

- **Relative Time is Your Friend:** Don't hardcode dates if you can use `earliest=-1d`, `latest=now`, etc. Your searches stay relevant as time moves on.
- **Macros:** For complex time calculations you reuse often, investigate Splunk's macro system. This is an advanced topic but can be powerful.
- **Visualizations Aid Understanding:** Sometimes, even a perfectly crafted search needs a great chart to make the point clear.

Additional Resources

- **Splunk Docs: Timechart Command:** https://docs.splunk.com/Documentation/Splunk/latest/SearchReference/Timechart
- **Splunk Docs: Search Macros:** https://docs.splunk.com/Documentation/Splunk/latest/SearchReference/WhatsInThisManual

Key Takeaways

- Mastering time isn't just about syntax, it's about asking the right questions of your data *across* time.
- Splunk lets you layer simple time-based searches to build sophisticated comparisons.
- The best analysis often combines time-focused searches with the ability to zoom in on the exact events behind an interesting data point.

Up Next

Fields are the soul of your data. Sometimes, Splunk extracts them automatically, but often, the most powerful insights come from defining those fields ourselves. Let's dive into advanced field extractions in the next chapter!

Practical: Field Extraction in Depth

Objectives

- Master the use of Regular Expressions (RegEx) for extractions.
- Extract fields from multi-line events.
- Handle data sources lacking consistent formatting.

Scenario 1: The Troublesome Firewall Log

Our firewall logs are a jumble. Example:

```
[10/15 08:25:13] DENY src=192.168.10.2
dst=8.8.8.8 proto=TCP SPT=53121 DPT=443
```

We Need: `timestamp`, `action`, `src`, `dst`, `proto`, `spt`, `dpt`

Solution

1. **Splunk Web:** "Settings" > "Fields" > "Field extractions" (Consider doing this at the sourcetype level)
2. **Extraction Type:** Regex. Let's build it piece by piece:

- `\[\(?(\d{2}/\d{2} \d{2}:\d{2}:\d{2})\]?` (Handles optional timestamp)
- `(\w+)` (Captures the action: DENY, ALLOW)
- `src=(\S+) dst=(\S+) proto=(\S+) SPT=(\d+) DPT=(\d+)` (The rest is more straightforward)

3. **Apply, Test, Iterate!** Splunk will preview if your regex works on sample events.

Scenario 2: The Stack Trace of Doom

Error logs include multi-line stack traces. We want the initial error message on one line, and the rest as `stack_trace`.

Solution:

1. **props.conf:** A key configuration file often edited by hand. Here's the magic:

```
[your_sourcetype]
SHOULD_LINEMERGE = true
BREAK_ONLY_BEFORE = ERROR
```

2. **Field Extraction:** Now search for 'ERROR' and extract subsequent fields as needed.

Scenario 3: When There's No Pattern

Sometimes data is just plain weird. Sample event:

```
Product ID: 12345 User: jsmith Session: 987654
(IP: 10.0.0.1)
```

Solution: The 'rex' Command Within a Search

```
| rex field=_raw "Product ID: (?<product_id>\d+)"
| rex field=_raw "User: (?<username>\w+)"
...
```

Important Notes

- **RegEx Mastery Takes Time:** Online regex testers are your friend! There are lots of resources to learn from.
- **props.conf and transforms.conf:** Vital for field extractions at data ingestion time. See the Splunk docs.
- **Tradeoffs:** Search-time extraction is flexible but adds overhead. Config files are efficient but require changes when log formats shift.

Additional Resources

- **Splunk Docs: Extract Fields with Regular Expressions:** https://docs.splunk.com/Documentation/Splunk/latest/Knowledge/ExtractfieldsinteractivelywithIFX
- **Splunk Docs: Regular Expression Cheatsheet:** https://docs.splunk.com/Documentation/Splunk/latest/SearchReference/rex
- **Online Regex Testers:** (Many available, e.g., https://regex101.com/)

Key Takeaways

- Field extractions are an investment – the cleaner your data, the better your searches!
- Splunk offers multiple ways to extract fields, choose the right tool for the job.
- Even the most chaotic data can usually be tamed with a combination of Splunk's features.

Up Next

We now have the power to search, extract fields, and leverage time. In the next chapters, we'll combine these skills and explore intermediate Splunk search concepts that supercharge your analysis capabilities!

Beyond Basics: Unleashing the Power of Intermediate Searches, Part 1

Objectives

- Master the `stats` command for powerful calculations.
- Learn how to use the `eval` command to create new fields and enhance calculations
- Apply the `where` command to filter with precision.

Scenario 1: Website Traffic Analysis (with a Twist)

Instead of just counting hits per URL, we want:

- **Top URLs by average bytes transferred:** Is a single URL hogging bandwidth?
- **Error Rate:** Percentage of requests with status codes >= 400.
- **Filter by Region:** Focus on a specific geographical area using an IP to Geolocation lookup (more on that later).

Starting Search

```
sourcetype=access_log
| lookup geoip clientip AS src_ip
| where region_name = "North America"
```

Step 1: Stats for the Win

```
... | stats sum(bytes) AS total_bytes, count BY uri_path
    | eval error_count=count(eval(status>=400))
    | eval error_rate=error_count/count * 100
    | sort - total_bytes
```

- `stats ... BY uri_path`: Groups calculations per URL.
- **sum(bytes) ... count**: Basic stats we'll need.
- **eval error_count...**: `eval` lets you make a field based on a condition.
- **eval error_rate...**: Calculates the percentage.

Step 2: Where to Filter

Use `where` for more complex filtering than a top-level search allows, especially after calculations:

- Examples:
    - `... | where error_rate > 10` (Only show URLs with high error rates)
    - `... | where total_bytes > 10000000` (Find bandwidth-heavy URLs)

Scenario 2: Security Incident Analysis

Find systems with multiple failed logins in a 5-minute window, followed by a successful one.

- **Statistical Outliers:** `| stats count by src_ip | eventstats avg(count) as avg_logins, stdev(count) as stdev | where count > ( avg_logins + stdev*2 )` (Identifies IPs with unusual login attempt counts)
- **Sequence Analysis:** This is where Splunk's `streamstats` command shines (a more advanced topic for a future chapter!)

Additional Resources

- **Splunk Docs: Stats Command:** https://docs.splunk.com/Documentation/Splunk/latest/SearchReference/Stats

- **Splunk Docs: Eval Command:**
  https://docs.splunk.com/Documentation/Splunk/latest/Searc
  hReference/Eval
- **Splunk Docs: Where Command:**
  https://docs.splunk.com/Documentation/Splunk/latest/Searc
  hReference/Where

Key Takeaways

- `stats` is how you aggregate – sums, averages, finding outliers, and more!
- `eval` creates calculated fields, opening up a world of analysis options.
- `where` allows for filtering on those calculated fields or complex combinations of logic.

Up Next

In Part 2, we'll cover more search commands that let you restructure your data, perform more advanced filtering and even correlate results from multiple searches.

Beyond Basics: Unleashing the Power of Intermediate Searches, Part 2

Objectives

- Understand the power of subsearches for more complex filtering and data enrichment.
- Use the `transaction` command to group events into logical units.
- Introduce the concept of correlated searches.

Scenario 1: Enriching Data with Lookups

We have firewall logs with source/destination IPs, but want:

- **Hostnames:** A CSV lookup file on our Splunk system maps IPs to hostnames.
- **Threat Level:** A subsearch against a threat intelligence platform (which can be modeled as a lookup)

The Search

```
sourcetype=firewall_log
| lookup hostnames ip AS src_ip OUTPUT host AS src_host
| lookup threat_intel src_ip OUTPUT threat_level
| where threat_level!="None"
```

- **Main Search:** Very simple. Most of the work happens in the lookups…
- **Lookup Basics:**
  - `lookup <lookupname> <field> AS <input_field> OUTPUT <new_field>`

- ○ Lookups often use CSV files on disk or other data sources Splunk can access
- **Subsearches:** Can also be used within lookup definitions for complex logic!

Scenario 2: Login Session Analysis

Goal: Find cases where the same user logs in from two wildly different locations within an hour.

The Search

```
sourcetype=authentication
| transaction user startswith="login_success" endswith="logout"
maxspan=1h
| where distance(src_ip1, src_ip2) > 2000
```

- **transaction:** Groups events together based on fields and conditions. This creates new fields like `duration`, and lets us correlate values within a transaction (e.g., `src_ip1` vs `src_ip2`)
- **Geospatial Functions:** Splunk has features to calculate distances! This would need the same GeoIP lookup from earlier examples.

Scenario 3: Correlating Across Sourcetypes

Goal: Alert when a web error is followed by a database server restart.

- **This is TRICKY!** Requires these concepts:
1. **Subsearch:** Find the timestamps of relevant web errors: [search sourcetype=web_error | head 10 | fields _time]
2. **Main Search:** Look for DB restarts, filtering on those timestamps:

```
sourcetype=db_logs action=restart
```

| where _time >= earliest_subsearch AND _time <= latest_subsearch

3. **Automation:** Put this into a scheduled report or a Splunk alert for real-world usage.

Additional Resources

- **Splunk Docs: Lookup Command:**
  https://docs.splunk.com/Documentation/Splunk/latest/SearchReference/Lookup
- **Splunk Docs: Transaction Command:**
  https://docs.splunk.com/Documentation/Splunk/latest/SearchReference/Transaction
- **Splunk Docs: Correlated Searches:**
  https://docs.splunk.com/Documentation/Splunk/latest/SearchTutorial/Correlatedsearches

Key Takeaways

- Subsearches let you nest one search within another, supercharging your filtering abilities.
- Lookups add context to events from external data sources.
- The `transaction` command helps when your analysis centers around events that span multiple log entries.
- Correlated searches are an advanced tool to find relationships across different datasets.

Up Next

Splunk offers a rich set of reporting and visualization tools. In the upcoming chapters, we'll learn to unlock them, building compelling dashboards to tell the story your data holds!

Section 6:
Crafting Visual Insights

Visualizing Data Dynamics: Grasping the Fundamentals

Objectives

- Understand the key types of visualizations and when to use them.
- Learn how to make visualizations clear and focused.
- Explore how color, titles, and labels play a role.

The Power of a Picture

- **Cognition:** Our brains process visual information much faster than raw numbers and tables.
- **Communication:** A well-made chart can convey insights to stakeholders or highlight areas for investigation, with far less explanation needed.
- **Exploration:** Visualizations themselves help you spot trends, outliers, or correlations that might be missed in textual data.

Types of Visualizations: Your Toolkit

1. **Time Series (Line Chart):** Classic choice for tracking metrics over time. See trends, seasonality, spikes.

2. **Bar Charts:** Comparing categories, seeing top/bottom values. Can be horizontal or vertical depending on the amount of text labeling needed.
3. **Pie/Donut Charts:** Parts of a whole. Use sparingly – humans aren't great at visually comparing angles.
4. **Tables:** Yes, even humble tables are visualizations! Best for precise values when the overall structure isn't the focus.
5. **Statistical:** Box plots, scatter plots… These shine when showing distributions or relationships between multiple variables.
6. **Gauges, Single Values:** Great for dashboard KPIs where you mainly care about the current status.

Scenario: Website Traffic Analysis

Let's make some visualizations of our `sourcetype=access_log` data:

- **Bad:** A pie chart with 20 slices, one for each top URL path. Hard to read!
- **Better:** A bar chart of the top 10 URLs by hit count. Immediately obvious what's popular.
- **Even Better:** A line chart showing total hits per minute over the past few days. Reveals traffic patterns the other charts miss.

Principles of Good Visualization

- **Focus:** Each chart should answer a specific question. Don't try to cram too much into one!
- **Clarity:**
  - Choose appropriate chart types (do you need to compare parts-of-whole, or trends over time?)
  - Labels and legends should be easy to understand.
  - Avoid 3D effects and excessive eye candy that distracts from the core data.

- **Color Consciously:**
  - Use color to highlight important elements or contrast groups.
  - Be mindful of color blindness – some palettes are harder to distinguish for some people.

Additional Resources

- **Splunk Docs: Visualization Reference:**
  https://docs.splunk.com/Documentation/Splunk/latest/Viz/Visualizationreference

Key Takeaways

- Choosing the right visualization is just as important as the underlying Splunk search.
- A simple, clear chart is better than a fancy but confusing one.
- Never underestimate the power of good titles and labeling to guide the viewer's interpretation.

Artistry in Analytics: Exploring Diverse Visualization Types

Objectives

- See beyond the standard charts. Learn about maps, geospatial analysis, and more.
- Understand how to customize visualizations for specific effects.
- Discover resources for more advanced visualization options.

Maps: When Location Matters

- **Prerequisites:** Often need geospatial data enrichment (IP to Lat/Lon, etc. – See earlier lookups chapter)
- **Use Cases:**
    - Visualizing security threats by origin.
    - Plotting store traffic by region on a custom map background.
    - Network device status overlaid on a physical floorplan.

Choropleth Maps

- Color-shaded regions where intensity represents some value.
- Great for visualizing website hits per country, average error rates by datacenter, etc.

Advanced Charting

- **Combo Charts:** Overlay lines and bars to compare related metrics with different scales. Example: Network bandwidth (line) and errors (bars) on the same timeline.

- **Trellis Layout (Small Multiples):** Breaks one chart into many panels based on a field. Great for comparing trends across server groups, product categories, etc., in a compact way.
- **Custom XML:** For those with serious design chops, Splunk dashboards have a raw XML mode for maximum control.

Scenario: Troubleshooting a Web Application

Imagine these searches:

1. `sourcetype=app_server response_time>500 | timechart avg(response_time) by endpoint_url`
2. `sourcetype=app_error | stats count by error_code, endpoint_url`

Possible Visualizations

- **Combo Chart:** Line for response time, bars for error count of the worst offender, over time. Immediately shows any correlation.
- **Table:** If precise numbers matter more than an at-a-glance visual comparison.
- **Trellis of Line Charts:** If we suspect some endpoints are consistently bad, a trellis with one small chart per endpoint lets us scan for patterns.

Customization is Key

- **Axis Labels and Scales:** Can make or break a chart. Does the Y-axis start at 0, or is it zoomed in to highlight variation? Logarithmic scales are sometimes necessary.
- **Colors:**
  - Sequential palettes (light to dark shades of one color) work well for magnitudes.
  - Diverging palettes highlight 'good' vs. 'bad' zones.

- ○ Qualitative palettes are for distinct categories
- **Annotations:** Can overlay events on charts. Mark deployments, outages, etc. for context.

Additional Resources

- **Splunk Docs: Chart Configuration Options:** https://docs.splunk.com/Documentation/Splunk/latest/Viz/ChartCustomizationOverview
- **Splunkbase:** Some apps offer extra visualization types https://splunkbase.splunk.com/

Key Takeaways

- Splunk's visualization power comes from its variety AND the ability to customize.
- Think about the story you want to tell, then choose a chart and tweak it to highlight what's important.
- Don't be afraid to experiment! Changing the visualization type can lead to whole new insights.

Constructing Data Frameworks: Unveiling the Realm of Data Models

Objectives

- Understand what Splunk Data Models are and why they matter.
- Learn how to create a basic Data Model.
- Explore the use of data models to power dashboards and reports.
- Discuss considerations for designing effective data models.

The Problem Data Models Solve

- **Raw Searches are Brittle:** A beautiful dashboard built on complex searches might break unexpectedly if the underlying log format changes, or you add a new field. This creates maintenance headaches and reduces trust in your reports.
- **Analysts vs. Search Experts:** You want less technical users to easily explore the data and build their own reports without having to master the intricacies of Splunk's search syntax.
- **Consistency:** It's easy for different analysts to calculate the same metric in slightly different ways. This leads to confusion ("Why does my dashboard show a higher error count than yours?"). Data models help solve this.

Data Models to the Rescue

- **Think of Them Like Database Tables:**
  - Each data model has a name (e.g., "Web Traffic", "Network Security Events").

- It defines a structured set of fields that can be extracted from your raw events. These fields can be calculated, renamed, looked up from external sources, or based directly on fields within your events.
- **Hierarchical:** Data models can inherit from others, adding more specialized fields as needed. This lets you create a base model with common attributes, and then extend it for specific use cases.
- **Accelerate Analysis:** Building dashboards and reports on top of a well-designed data model is incredibly fast. Often, you can get the visualizations you need with very simple searches, or sometimes no search at all!

Scenario: Website Analytics

Imagine you need comprehensive website analytics, but your data sources are a mix of web server access logs, custom application logs, and even a database table with user demographics. A data model can unify all this.

1. **Base Data Model ('Web Events') Might Include Fields Like:**
   - timestamp
   - client_ip
   - uri_path
   - status_code
   - user_agent
   - session_id
2. **Child Data Model ('Web Errors'):**
   - Inherits from the base model
   - Adds fields:
     - is_error (Boolean calculated from `status_code`)
     - error_severity (Categorizes errors for easier grouping)

3. **Another Child Model ('Web Purchases'):**
   - ○ Also inherits from 'Web Events'
   - ○ Adds fields:
     - ■ product_id
     - ■ purchase_amount
     - ■ user_id (This might be looked up from that user demographics database)

How to Create Data Models

- **Splunk Web:** "Settings" -> "Data models"
- **Mostly Visual:** Splunk guides you through selecting your data source (usually one or more sourcetypes), previewing how events will be mapped, and defining field transformations.
- **Behind the Scenes:** Data models do generate complex Splunk searches to accelerate data at reporting time. Luckily, you're shielded from most of that!

Using Your Data Model

- **Pivot Tool:** Easily switch from raw events to your data model. Your defined fields now show up as choices for building reports.
- **Dashboards:** Many visualization panels can be built directly on the data model, simplifying the underlying searches.
- **Reports:** Splunk can translate dashboard panels based on a Data Model into optimized searches for regular report generation.

Key Considerations for Data Model Design

- **Naming:** Descriptive names for models and fields are crucial for self-service usage by others.
- **Balance:** Too granular, and you have a proliferation of models. Too broad, and they become hard to use.

- **Documentation:** Splunk lets you add descriptions to data models and fields. This is vital for long-term maintainability!

Additional Resources

- **Splunk Docs: Introduction to Data Models:** https://docs.splunk.com/Documentation/Splunk/latest/Knowl edge/Introductiontodatamodels
- **Splunk Docs: Create Data Models:** https://docs.splunk.com/Documentation/Splunk/latest/Knowl edge/Understanddatamodels

Key Takeaways

- Data models are an investment that pays off with more robust, user-friendly, and maintainable Splunk dashboards and reports
- Think about the questions you want to answer, and design your data models to support those analyses.
- Start with a few core data models and iterate as your reporting needs evolve.

Up Next

Now that we have a foundation with data models, let's explore how to turn them into actionable insights through Splunk's powerful reporting features and scheduled reports.

Reporting Renaissance: Empowering Insights and Alerts

Objectives

- Understand the key differences between dashboards and reports.
- Learn to create and schedule reports.
- Explore delivery options like email and webhooks.
- Master the art of scheduled alerts for proactive monitoring.

Dashboards vs. Reports: A Tale of Two Tools

- **Dashboards:**
  - Interactive, real-time focused, great for exploration
  - Users might need some Splunk search fluency to get the most out of them.
  - Often designed for a screen, not print.
- **Reports:**
  - Can be scheduled to run on intervals (every hour, daily, etc.)
  - Output can be embedded in emails, attached as PDFs, even trigger actions in external systems.
  - Easier for non-Splunk experts to consume.

Scenario 1: Executive Summary

You need a weekly PDF attached to an email, summarizing top website errors, slow pages, and traffic by country. This is a REPORT.

Scenario 2: Security Operations Center (SOC)

The SOC has a giant dashboard showing a real-time view of potential attacks. When certain critical thresholds are exceeded, the system needs to send an alert to PagerDuty to wake up the on-call engineer. This is an ALERT.

Creating Reports in Splunk

1. **Base It on a Search, or Use a Visualization:** Often, you'll start with a dashboard panel and click "Save As Report"
2. **Scheduling:** Set the frequency. Consider if it needs to run on an exact schedule (midnight daily), or just regularly (every 6 hours).
3. **Delivery:**
   - Email (Inline, PDF, CSV Attached, etc.)
   - Run a Script (for advanced integrations)
4. **Permissions:** Who is allowed to see and modify the report?

Configuring Alerts

1. **Base It on a Search:** Your search defines the criteria to trigger the alert (e.g., `sourcetype=firewall action=block | stats count by src_ip | where count > 50`)
2. **Conditions:**
   - Per Result: Alert on each event
   - Number of Results: Alert when a search returns more than X matching events.
   - Customize: Trigger based on complex field calculations in your results.
3. **Schedule:**
   - How often to run the search? Real-time alerts are possible but use with caution!
   - Throttling: Suppress repeated alerts if the issue persists, to avoid flooding inboxes.
4. **Actions:**
   - Email
   - Webhook: Incredibly powerful for ticketing systems, custom apps, etc.

      ◦   Script (for the brave!)

Additional Tips

- **Report Acceleration:** Data models (see the previous chapter) can significantly speed up report generation.
- **Alert Fatigue is Real:** Too many noisy alerts, and people start ignoring them. Tune carefully!
- **Documentation:** Especially for critical alerts, include troubleshooting steps or links to a team wiki right in the alert content. Saves precious time during an incident.

Additional Resources

- **Splunk Docs: Scheduled Reports:** https://docs.splunk.com/Documentation/Splunk/latest/Repor t/Schedulerreports
- **Splunk Docs: Alerts:** https://docs.splunk.com/Documentation/Splunk/latest/Alert/ Aboutalerts

Key Takeaways

- Reports extend the value of a dashboard by delivering insights to stakeholders who may not even log in to Splunk directly.
- Alerts turn Splunk into a monitoring system, ensuring timely response to problems.
- Mastering reporting and alerts bridges the gap between those who analyze data in Splunk and those who need to act on those insights.

Up Next

We've covered a lot of ground! In the next chapters, we'll delve into some more specialized visualization techniques, starting with harnessing the power of the Pivot interface.

Pivot Wizardry: Harnessing the Pivot Tool for Insights

Objectives

- Understand when and why to choose the Pivot interface.
- Master how to structure and manipulate Pivot tables.
- Explore the various ways Pivots can fuel insightful dashboards.

Pivot vs. Regular Tables

- **Standard Tables:** Show rows of events. Good for detailed lists, but hard to see trends across many values.
- **Pivot:**
  - Summarizes data into a matrix
  - One field becomes your rows, another becomes columns, and you fill the cells with calculations (count, average, sum, etc.)
  - Handles large, potentially messy data more effectively

Scenario: Website Errors Over Time

Imagine you need this:

Hour of Day	HTTP 404 Errors	HTTP 500 Errors	HTTP 503 Errors	...
00:00 - 00:59	1234	35	0	...

01:00 - 01:59	578	22	13	...
...				

The Pivot Approach

1. **Base Search:** `sourcetype=access_log` (ideally, status codes would already be extracted as a field)
2. **Open the Pivot Interface:** Often easily accessible from a search results table visualization.
3. **Rows:** `timechart span=1h count by status_code` (We group by time and status code)
4. **Columns:** `status_code` (Each status code becomes its own column)
5. **Values:** `count` (We simply count events in each cell)

Making Pivots Work for You

- **Filtering:** Done before pivoting. Reduces the amount of data the Pivot has to summarize.
- **Split Rows/Columns:** Create nested groupings (e.g., error count per URL path, further split by country).
- **Calculations:** Besides 'count', you can sum, average, find the min/max, etc.
- **Cosmetic:** Rename those auto-generated column names to something user-friendly!

Pivots in Dashboards

While you CAN build an entire dashboard out of one giant Pivot, it's usually better to:

- **Create Multiple, Focused Pivots:** One for error trends, one for traffic per country… Users digest smaller chunks of data better.
- **Pair Them with Other Visuals:** Show a line chart with total errors over time, then a Pivot below drilling down into error types. This provides context.

Additional Resources

- **Splunk Docs: Pivot Command:** https://docs.splunk.com/Documentation/Splunk/latest/SearchReference/Pivot
- **Splunk Docs: Using Pivot:** https://docs.splunk.com/Documentation/Splunk/latest/Pivot/AboutPivot

Key Takeaways:

- The Pivot is your best friend when you need to compare many categories along another dimension (often time).
- Start with a simple Pivot, then experiment with splitting rows/columns or more complex cell calculations.
- Pivots are incredibly powerful, but don't neglect the overall presentation of the data when designing your dashboards!

Up Next

Now that you're armed with Pivot mastery, let's put it to practice! In the upcoming practical chapters, we'll tackle real-world dashboard building scenarios using the Pivot alongside other visualization tools.

Practical: Crafting Dashboards with Pivot, Part 2

Objectives

- Explore options for enhanced Pivot readability on dashboards.
- Use color, formatting, and annotations to guide interpretation.
- Learn to incorporate Pivot results with other visualizations for a holistic view.

Scenario: Website Performance Analysis

In the previous chapter, we likely built some Pivots around:

- Average page load time by URL path, split by device type (desktop, mobile, etc.)
- HTTP error breakdowns by country
- Number of slow database queries executed, split by web server

Now, let's turn these into a compelling dashboard!

Pivot Presentation

- **Cell Highlighting:** Splunk lets you conditionally format cells based on values. e.g., Longest load times get a red background, easily drawing the eye.
- **Number Formatting:** Raw counts are good, but percentages or more readable durations (3.2s vs. 3215ms) improve comprehension.
- **Totals:** Consider adding row or column totals where they make sense for comparison.

- **Limit Row/Column Count:** Can the user filter the Pivot, or do you pre-slice it to the top 10 URL paths, etc.? A giant Pivot is overwhelming.

Combining Visualizations

1. **Big Number + Pivot:** Show the current total number of errors as a single value display, then the Pivot below breaks it down.
2. **Time Chart + Pivots:** A line chart showing overall website traffic over time. Below it, two pivots: one for top URLs, one for top countries. This lets viewers see if a traffic spike correlates with problems in a specific location.
3. **Pivot as a Filter:** In some cases, clicking a cell in a Pivot can be used to drill down into detailed results on another part of the dashboard.

Beyond the Data Table

- **Titles:** Never underestimate the power of a clear dashboard title and descriptive labels above each visualization.
- **Help Text:** A panel with brief instructions or links to a wiki with definitions of key terms can be a lifesaver, especially if non-technical stakeholders use the dashboard.
- **Annotations:** Did you deploy a new version of the website? Mark it on charts. Did an outage occur? Adding that context helps connect the dots.

Additional Resources

- **Splunk Docs: Improve Your Tables and Charts:** https://docs.splunk.com/Documentation/Splunk/latest/Viz/ChartCustomizationIntro

Key Takeaways

- A technically perfect Pivot won't achieve its purpose if users are confused by the presentation.
- Put yourself in the shoes of someone seeing this dashboard for the first time – is it intuitive?
- Think of dashboards as a story told with data. Arrangement of visualizations, along with clear labeling, guides the narrative.

Up Next

Now let's dive into general dashboard design principles, turning your analytical prowess into dashboards that are both informative and visually appealing.

Practical: Exploring Dashboard Craftsmanship, Part 1

Objectives

- Understand principles of layout and visual hierarchy to guide viewers.
- Master color usage for clarity and emphasis.
- Learn the art of whitespace and why it matters.
- Explore techniques to ensure dashboards are accessible and colorblind-friendly.

Think Like a Designer (Just a Little!)

Great dashboards follow some basic design rules, even if you don't have a graphic design background:

- **Visual Hierarchy:** The most important metrics should catch the eye first. This can be achieved through size, color, and placement. Consider:
    - **Size:** Larger elements naturally draw more attention.
    - **Placement:** Top/center positions tend to dominate visually, while bottom corners are less prominent.
- **Grouping:** Related charts or visualizations should be placed near each other. Aligning elements along a subtle grid creates a sense of order and helps viewers make connections.
- **Flow:** Guide the eye in a logical way. Think about the typical questions someone would ask when viewing the dashboard, and structure the layout to support that thought process.

Scenario: Security Incident Dashboard

Let's imagine this needs to be immediately understandable by both an analyst digging into an alert and an executive checking high-level status:

1. **Top Row:**
   - Single Value: Current number of active high-severity alerts (Big, bold, maybe red if the number is non-zero)
   - Map: Location of attacks in the past hour (visual and immediate)
2. **Middle Row:**
   - Line Chart: Alert volume trend over the past day. Are things escalating?
   - Pivot: Top blocked source IP addresses, to spot patterns
3. **Bottom Row:**
   - Pivot or Table: Recent alerts with key details, clickable for detailed investigation

Color Theory for Dashboards

- **Less is More:** Start with a simple palette (2-3 main colors). Too much color becomes chaotic and makes it harder to establish a visual language.
- **Meaningful Color:**
  - Sequential palettes for magnitudes (light blue = low count, dark blue = high count).
  - Diverging palettes to clearly highlight 'good' vs. 'bad' zones of a chart.
  - Qualitative for distinct categories (error types each get a different, clearly distinguishable color)
- **Accessibility:** Consider viewers with color blindness. Check your dashboard with a colorblindness simulator tool online. Some key tips:
  - Use patterns or textures in addition to color to differentiate elements.

- Ensure sufficient contrast between text and background, even in color-deficient modes.

The Power of Whitespace

- **Margins:** Don't let panels bleed to the very edge of the screen. Give your visualizations some breathing room.
- **Spacing Between Elements:** Reduces visual clutter and lets the important parts 'pop'.
- **Don't Fear the Empty Space:** Sometimes, removing a less-critical chart or visualization gives the important ones room to breathe. Remember, it's about clarity and focus.

Additional Resources

- **Splunk Dashboard Examples App:** https://splunkbase.splunk.com/app/1603/ . Even if you don't install them, it's great inspiration.

Key Takeaways

- A good dashboard isn't just about the data; it's about how the data is presented.
- A few thoughtful tweaks to layout, color, and spacing can dramatically improve how quickly insights are grasped.
- Don't be afraid to experiment! Splunk allows for quick edits and previews. Iterate on your design.

Up Next

In the next part of this series, we'll delve into techniques for making dashboards dynamic, allowing users to slice and dice the data without needing to know complex Splunk search syntax.

Practical: Exploring Dashboard Craftsmanship, Part 2

Objectives

- Learn to use dashboard input elements (dropdowns, text boxes, etc.) for filtering.
- Understand how tokens can pass data between dashboard panels.
- Explore techniques to make dashboards adaptable to different time ranges.

Power to the Users (Within Limits)

Interactive dashboards give users flexibility, but it's a balancing act:

- **Too Rigid:** No one will use it if they can't adjust the view to their needs.
- **Too Flexible:** Might turn into an analysis rabbit hole. Consider your audience and the dashboard's primary purpose.

Input Types

Splunk offers several ways for users to provide input:

- **Dropdown:** Great for selecting from a predefined list: server names, countries, product categories…
- **Text Input:** Freeform text. Use with caution – a typo can break searches! Sometimes better for advanced users who know your data.
- **Time Range Picker:** Essential. Let users switch between last hour, day, week, etc.

- **More Advanced:** Radio buttons, multi-select (for picking multiple categories at once), and more exist.

Scenario: Troubleshooting Tools

Imagine a dashboard for engineers supporting an online game. Key components:

1. **Dropdown:** Select a specific server instance
2. **Time Range:** Standard Splunk picker on the top
3. **Line chart:** Errors per minute, faceted (separate line) for each major game subsystem
4. **Table:** Recent high-severity errors for the SELECTED server

Tokens: Your Secret Weapon

- **What?:** Think of them as variables you define on the dashboard level. E.g., `$server_name$`
- **In Searches:** Instead of hardcoding a server, use the token:
  `sourcetype=game_errors`
  `server="$server_name$"`
- **Populated by Inputs:** When a user picks from the dropdown, it sets the value of that token.
- **Result:** Panels 3 and 4 automatically update, no need for the user to edit multiple searches!

Dynamic Time Handling

Make sure your visualizations adapt correctly when a user picks "Last 24 hours" vs. "Last 7 days":

- **Relative Time Modifiers:** Your friend! `earliest=-24h@h latest=now` is far better than fixed dates.
- **Base Searches:** If you built panels correctly, they should "just work".

- **Testing is Key:** Click through all your time range options. Do charts rescale their axes? Do time-based calculations still make sense?

Additional Tips

- **Link Separate Dashboards:** Instead of one monster dashboard, break it up and provide links to drill down. Example: Main overview links to a Server Detail dashboard, pre-filtering to that server using tokens.
- **Simple XML Mode:** For truly advanced customization, dashboards can be edited as raw XML. This unlocks even more possibilities but requires some deeper Splunk knowledge.

Additional Resources

- **Splunk Docs: Use Input Elements on Dashboards:** https://docs.splunk.com/Documentation/Splunk/latest/Viz/tokens
- **Splunk Docs: Dashboard Examples:** https://splunkbase.splunk.com/app/1603/ (Provides inspiration and XML you might be able to learn from)

Key Takeaways

- A pinch of interactivity goes a LONG way in dashboard usability.
- Tokens are a powerful tool to link panels together.
- Always design with different time ranges in mind.

Up Next

To complete the picture, we need to cover how Data Models, introduced in a previous chapter, make dashboards even more powerful and user-friendly.

Practical: Building Dynamic Data Models, Part 1

Objectives

- Understand the key benefits of building Data Models for dashboards.
- Learn to create a simple Data Model through the Splunk web interface.
- Explore how to use tokens within Data Models for enhanced adaptability.

Why Bother with Data Models Again?

- **User-friendliness:** Instead of raw field names, your Pivot interface and dashboard inputs can show the nice names you define in the data model!
- **Centrally Managed:** Update field calculations or aliases in the Data Model, and those changes propagate to ALL dashboards using it. Huge time saver.
- **Performance:** For complex dashboards, doing certain calculations at indexing time (which Data Models enable) means reports and visualizations run lightning-fast.

Scenario: Website Analytics Deep Dive

Let's extend the website analysis example to illustrate the power of Data Models:

- **Raw Data:** You have `access_log` data, maybe some custom logs. Fields include things like `http_status`, `bytes_sent`, `page_url`, `referrer`, and more.
- **Goal:** A dashboard with filters for country, device type (from user-agent) and the ability to analyze errors, traffic, and conversions (which is defined in a lookup, let's say.).

Building the Data Model

1. **Data Model Name:** "Web Traffic Analysis" (descriptive!)
2. **Base Search:** Here, you select your sourcetype(s). NOTE: You can further refine this with a search, but try to make your base search as broadly useful as possible.
3. **Root Event:** Choose this wisely. It impacts how the model works. Often the same as your base search, but it could be narrowed further.
4. **Fields:** Let's do some magic:
   - **Rename:** Change `http_status` to "Status Code"
   - **Categorize:** `page_url` gets a category of "Page"
   - **Calculated:**
     - `is_error=if(Status_Code>=400, "Yes", "No")`
     - `size_mb=bytes_sent / 1024 / 1024` (for more readable sizes)
   - **Lookups:** Join to that lookup defining conversions. Let's call that new field `is_conversion`

Using Your Masterpiece

- **Pivot:** Now it's "Average Page Load Time by Page" instead of cryptic field names.
- **Dashboard Inputs:** Dropdowns will populate with the descriptive names you defined.
- **Token Magic:** If a dropdown sets country, your Data Model search can have a `WHERE country="$country$"` constraint.

Additional Notes

- **Child Data Models:** These can add even more refined calculations or narrow the focus while inheriting everything from the parent.

- **Performance vs. Flexibility:** Data Models add some overhead. For extremely high-volume data sets, sometimes a little less acceleration is accepted in favor of more flexible on-the-fly calculations.

Additional Resources

- **Splunk Docs: Data Model Creation:**
  https://docs.splunk.com/Documentation/Splunk/latest/Knowledge/DataModelOverview

Key Takeaways

- Data Models are an investment: a little more work upfront leads to better dashboards down the line.
- Think beyond just renaming fields. Clever calculations and lookups done within the Data Model supercharge your analysis possibilities.
- Even a simple Data Model will usually make dashboards significantly easier for non-Splunk-experts to use.

Up Next

While we covered the core concepts, Data Models have even more advanced capabilities! In the next part, we'll tackle more sophisticated Data Model building to further refine how your data can be analyzed.

Practical: Building Dynamic Data Models, Part 2

Objectives

- Learn how to organize fields within a Data Model into hierarchies.
- Explore the use of regular expressions for field extraction within Data Models.
- Understand how to constrain Data Models for specific use cases.

Beyond the Basics

Let's build upon our previous website analytics example and address some real-world complexities:

Scenario: URL Chaos

- Your `page_url` field is a mess: `/product.php?id=123`, `/article/some-long-title`, etc.
- Goal: Analyze traffic by page categories or extract things like product IDs, not the whole raw URL.

Hierarchies to the Rescue

1. **In your "Web Traffic Analysis" Data Model, go to Fields -> Field Extractions**
2. **New Extraction:** Let's get the page category:
   - **Type:** Regex.
   - **Extraction:** Something like `\/(?<page_category>[^\/\?]+)` (captures the first segment after the "/")
   - **Apply to:** Page

3. **Create More Extractions:** Maybe one for product id using a more tailored regex.

Benefits

- **Cleaner Pivots:** Now you pivot by 'Page Category' instead of a mess of URLs.
- **Inheritance:** Child Data Models automatically get these new, cleaned-up fields!

Constraints: When to Narrow the Scope

1. **"Web Errors" Child Model:**
    - **Base Search on Data Model:** Select the 'Web Traffic Analysis' model
    - **Additional Constraint:** `is_error="Yes"`
2. **Why It Matters:**
    - Performance: Calculations on error events are far faster, as the parent model already did a bunch of the work.
    - Focus: Dashboards based on "Web Errors" won't be cluttered with options irrelevant to errors.

Regular Expressions – Your Superpower

If regular expressions are new to you, prepare for a learning curve. But the effort is worth it!

- **Data Model field extractions are the perfect place to practice:** You get immediate visual feedback if your regex works.
- **Splunk Docs have a reference, but there are also tons of online regex resources and testers**

Additional Notes

- **Field Aliases:** Sometimes a simpler solution than regex! Just rename a field to something user-friendly, no calculation needed.
- **Eval** statements within Data Models: For truly advanced logic (though use with caution due to performance impact)

Additional Resources

- **Splunk Docs: Regular Expressions:** https://docs.splunk.com/Documentation/Splunk/latest/SearchReference/Rex
- **Online Regex Testers:** Many available, e.g., https://regex101.com/

Key Takeaways

- A messy field can be broken down into meaningful parts within the Data Model itself.
- Child data models let you create specialized views without repeating all the base transformations.
- Data models aren't JUST for beginners. Advanced Splunk users lean on them heavily to organize their data.

Wrapping Up Our Dashboard Journey

We've covered a LOT of ground. You should feel empowered to go from raw log data to compelling, interactive dashboards that guide insights. Remember, Splunk is powerful, so take things step by step, and don't be afraid to experiment!

Section 7:

Mastery of Advanced Concepts

Orchestrating Deployment: Managing Servers and Forwarders

Objectives

- Understand the key components of a distributed Splunk environment.
- Learn deployment best practices for scalability, reliability, and security.
- Grasp concepts like forwarder management, deployment servers, and the roles of different Splunk components.

Beyond a Single Server

While smaller Splunk deployments might run entirely on one machine, the true power of Splunk in an enterprise setting comes from its ability to scale across multiple servers. Let's break down the key players:

- **Indexers:** The backbone of your data storage. These are where logs and metrics get stored long-term and where most searches run. A cluster of indexers provides redundancy (keeping your data safe if a server fails) and allows you to handle huge volumes of data.
- **Search Heads:** These provide the user interface for Splunk – dashboards, reports, search bar, etc. Distributing multiple

search heads is especially important if you have many users or those dashboards contain complex visualizations that demand computing power.

- **Heavy Forwarders:** These act as a middle layer between your lightweight Universal Forwarders and the indexers. Heavy forwarders might do complex data parsing, filtering, or routing that you don't want to burden your indexers with.
- **Universal Forwarders:** The workhorses of the Splunk world! These lightweight agents can be installed on virtually any machine that generates log data – Windows and Linux servers, network devices, cloud infrastructure... you name it.

Deployment Planning: Thinking Ahead

Scaling Splunk isn't just about throwing more hardware at the problem. Consider these questions:

- **Capacity:** How much data are you ingesting each day? How long do you need to retain it for analysis? These factors directly impact the size and design of your indexer cluster.
- **Redundancy:** Hardware failures *will* happen. Design your Splunk environment so that the loss of a single server, even an important one, doesn't cripple your ability to gather and analyze data.
- **Network:** Forwarders sending data to indexers can consume significant network bandwidth. Plan accordingly! Consider tiering your deployment: local forwarders send to regional aggregators, which then send to a central indexer cluster.

Enter: the Deployment Server

- **Purpose:** Think of it as mission control for your army of Universal Forwarders. This centralized server lets you manage configuration settings for vast numbers of forwarders, ensuring consistency and ease of updates.

- **How It Works**
  - ○ You define 'classes' of forwarders (e.g., "Web Servers", "Database Servers", "Network Devices").
  - ○ Each class gets assigned apps (for parsing data) and configuration settings (which logs to collect, where to send them, etc.).
  - ○ Forwarders regularly check in with the deployment server to see if there are updates for them.

Benefits of the Deployment Server

1. **Consistency:** Need to update how you parse Apache logs? Make the change on the deployment server, and it can be automatically rolled out to hundreds or thousands of forwarders.
2. **Version Control (Kinda):** The deployment server keeps a history of what configuration was sent to which forwarders. This gives you some ability to roll back changes if needed.
3. **Scaling:** Managing forwarders manually on a large scale is a recipe for errors and frustration. The deployment server is essential.

Additional Considerations

- **Monitoring the Monitoring:** Build dashboards to monitor the health of your Splunk deployment itself! Track indexing volume, search performance, forwarder status, and more.
- **Distributed Search:** With a properly configured setup, users don't need to know exactly which indexer holds their data. A search head can seamlessly query indexers across your entire Splunk environment.
- **Indexer Clustering:** This is an advanced topic, but it provides the highest level of data redundancy and complex

search capabilities. A cluster involves multiple indexer machines working in unison.

Additional Resources

- **Splunk Docs: About Distributed Deployment:** https://docs.splunk.com/Documentation/Splunk/latest/Updating/Distributeddeploymentoverview
- **Splunk Docs: Deployment Server:** https://docs.splunk.com/Documentation/Splunk/latest/Updating/Aboutdeploymentserver

Key Takeaways

- Splunk's distributed architecture allows it to scale from a small departmental tool to an enterprise-wide log management platform.
- The Deployment Server is crucial for managing large numbers of Universal Forwarders.
- Planning your deployment around capacity, redundancy, and network considerations will ensure that your Splunk environment runs smoothly as it grows.

Up Next

Managing users and their permissions is another aspect of operating a secure and well-organized Splunk environment – let's explore that next!

Gatekeeping Access: Delving into User Management and Authentication, Part 1

Objectives

- Understand Splunk's concept of roles and how they grant permissions.
- Learn how to create and manage users within Splunk.
- Explore the basics of authentication mechanisms supported by Splunk.

Why Security Isn't Optional

- **Compliance:** Regulations like HIPAA, PCI-DSS, and others often mandate access controls and audit trails of who accessed what data. Splunk helps you meet those requirements.
- **Data Integrity:** Mistakes happen! A well-designed role system minimizes the risk of an accidental mass deletion of important logs by an inexperienced user.
- **Visibility Limits:** Not everyone needs to see everything. Restrict access to sensitive data sources (like HR records) or dashboards containing confidential business metrics.

Roles: Building Blocks of Permissions

- **What Are Roles?:** A named collection of capabilities within Splunk. Example roles might be "Developer", "Security Analyst", "Network Operations Viewer".
- **Not Just for People:** Some internal Splunk processes have roles, and system-generated dashboards may depend on specific roles existing.

- **Built-In vs. Custom:** Splunk ships with some essential roles (`admin`, `power`, `user`). You'll almost always create your own as well.
- **Capabilities:** A detailed list, but they boil down to things like:
    - Can the user create searches? Save reports? Install apps?
    - What indexes can they see?
    - Can they edit system settings?

Managing Users in Splunk

Typically, you'll do most of this through the Splunk web interface. Only the `admin` role can manage other users.

1. **Creating Users:**
    - Username, password, and their real name (Good for accountability!)
    - Default Role: Pick one, but this can be changed later.
    - Timezone (Affects how dates/times are displayed for that user)
2. **Assigning Roles:** A user can have multiple roles. All the capabilities from each assigned role are combined.
3. **Passwords:**
    - Splunk can enforce basic complexity rules (length, characters, etc.).
    - Ideally, don't manage passwords within Splunk at all, but integrate with your company's existing authentication system (more on that later).

Authentication: Who Are You, Really?

- **Built-in (usernames/passwords stored by Splunk):** Fine for small deployments, but gets cumbersome to manage at scale.

- **LDAP:** Connect Splunk to your Active Directory or similar system. Leverages your existing user accounts, groups, and likely password policies.
- **SAML:** For single sign-on (SSO) integrations. Users authenticate with services like Okta or OneLogin, then get seamless access to Splunk.
- **Scripted:** For the truly adventurous, you can hook Splunk up to a custom authentication system using scripts.

Authentication Notes

- **Roles STILL Matter:** Even if you authenticate with LDAP, you map those external groups/users to roles within Splunk to control their fine-grained permissions.
- **Best Fit:** For most businesses, LDAP or SAML are the recommended ways to go.

Additional Resources

- **Splunk Docs: Manage Users and Roles:**
  https://docs.splunk.com/Documentation/Splunk/latest/Securi ty/Addusersandassignroles
- **Splunk Docs: Authentication Methods:**
  https://docs.splunk.com/Documentation/Splunk/latest/Securi ty/Authenticationoverview

Key Takeaways

- Splunk's role system provides granular control over what different users can see and do.
- Think about your users and the level of access they truly need before creating custom roles.
- Integrating Splunk with your existing authentication system (LDAP or SAML) often makes both security and user management significantly easier.

Up Next

In Part 2, we'll dive into more advanced aspects of roles and explore how authentication settings can impact things like scripted inputs and even some apps!

Gatekeeping Access: Delving into User Management and Authentication, Part 2

Objectives

- Understand the inheritance of role-based permissions within Splunk.
- Learn how authentication choices impact other aspects of Splunk.
- Explore more advanced role customization for fine-grained control.

Inheritance Matters: Where Permissions Come From

Permissions in Splunk can be granted at several levels, forming a hierarchy:

1. **System Level:** The base capabilities of built-in roles (admin, power, etc.)
2. **App Level:** Individual Splunk apps can define their own roles which only control access to things within that app.
3. **Object Level:** Saved searches, reports, dashboards, etc., can have specific sharing settings (private to just the owner, visible to users with a certain role, and so on).

Example: Helpdesk Dashboard

- A "Helpdesk Analyst" role:
    - Can search indexes containing application logs
    - Has access to an app called "Troubleshooting Tools"
    - Can view a specific dashboard named "Web Server Errors", but cannot edit it.

Authentication's Hidden Impact

- **Scripted Inputs:** If a data input script relies on credentials, those might need to be stored within Splunk or managed in a way the user has access to (depending on your authentication setup).
- **Some Apps:** May require Splunk's built-in user management since they deeply tie into user-specific settings or storage. This is uncommon, but something to be aware of if using lesser-known or custom-built apps.
- **External Validation (LDAP)** If your directory server is down, logins might fail even with the correct password! Plan for this in your incident response procedures.

Advanced Role Techniques

Let's get more granular! While the Splunk UI is good for the basics, sometimes you need to fine-tune capabilities that it doesn't expose.

- **Editing roles.conf:** This configuration file offers more options than the UI. **Caution:** Easy to make mistakes, so work on a copy, and validate carefully!
- **Selected Fields:** Limit a role to seeing ONLY certain fields within events, even if they technically have access to the data. Use case: Masking sensitive data like credit card numbers.
- **Search Filters:** A hard limit on what data a role can even retrieve from your indexes. Use case: Regional admins only see data for their geographic area.

When "Out of the Box" Roles Don't Fit

- **Start with a Base:** Don't create roles entirely from scratch. Begin with a close-fitting built-in role, or clone an existing custom one, then modify it.

- **Principle of Least Privilege:** Give users the bare minimum permissions to do their jobs. Reduces risks of both accidents and malicious actions.
- **Audit:** Sadly, no great UI for this. You may need to do creative searches to sce who did what or leverage internal Splunk logs (`_audit`) for tracking changes to users and roles.

Additional Resources

- **Splunk Docs: Search Filters and Role Permissions:** https://docs.splunk.com/Documentation/Splunk/latest/Security/Searchfiltersearches
- **Splunk Docs: roles.conf Specification:** https://docs.splunk.com/Documentation/Splunk/latest/Admin/Rolesconf

Key Takeaways

- Splunk offers multiple layers of access control, from broad roles down to restrictions on specific objects.
- Your choice of authentication method impacts more than just how users log in. Consider it during implementation planning.
- Use caution when going beyond basic role management through the user interface, as mistakes can have unintended consequences.

Up Next

Splunk's power comes in large part from its ability to be customized. Configuration files are at the heart of this. Let's start demystifying those in the next chapter!

Configuration Chronicles: Unraveling Configuration File Essentials, Part 1

Objectives

- Understand the structure and purpose of Splunk configuration files.
- Learn the key configuration files that control core Splunk behavior.
- Explore how to make changes to configuration files safely.
- Discover how configuration settings interact across different levels.

Splunk's Backbone: More Than Meets the Eye

While Splunk has a beautiful web interface, behind the scenes, it's driven by plain text configuration files. These determine everything from:

- **Data Inputs:** Where does Splunk get logs?
- **Field Extractions:** How are raw events broken into meaningful fields?
- **Search Behavior:** Timezone defaults, search limits…
- **Visuals:** Colors of charts (surprisingly, often defined in these files!)
- **…and SO much more**

Where to Find Them

- Splunk splits its config files into these main locations:
    - `$SPLUNK_HOME/etc/system/default/`: Core settings out of the box. Be VERY cautious changing these.

- ○ `$SPLUNK_HOME/etc/system/local/`: Where you primarily override defaults and put your customizations.
- ○ `$SPLUNK_HOME/etc/apps/<appname>/default`: App-specific defaults
- ○ `$SPLUNK_HOME/etc/apps/<appname>/local`: App-specific customizations

File Format: .conf

Splunk configuration files use a format called 'stanzas'. Example (`inputs.conf`):

```
[monitor://C:\Windows\System32\*.log]
disabled = false
index = windows_logs
sourcetype = windows_system
```

- **[monitor:...]:** This defines a stanza named 'monitor://C:\Windows\System32*.log', which configures a file monitoring data input.
- **disabled = false:** A key-value setting within that stanza.

Essential Files to Know

Let's focus on some files likely found in `system/local`:

- **inputs.conf:** Data inputs (files, network ports, etc.)
- **props.conf:** Key to parsing data! Controls how fields are extracted, timezones, etc.
- **transforms.conf:** Used for advanced pre-indexing modifications – like calculating new fields, or lookups.
- **indexes.conf:** Defines your indexes (where data is stored long-term) and their retention settings.

Making Changes

- **Splunk Web:** Often the best choice. Manages updates safely and guides you through valid options.
- **Manual Editing:** Sometimes necessary.
  - ○ **SAFETY:** Make backups before changing things!
  - ○ **Restart Required:** Splunk usually needs a restart to pick up on configuration file changes.

Configuration Hierarchy

Understanding how settings are applied is crucial to avoid surprises:

1. **System Defaults:** The foundation.
2. **App Defaults:** Can override system settings.
3. **Local Changes:** Your customizations have the final say!
4. **Search Time:** Some settings can even be applied dynamically within a specific search command, overriding what's in the configuration files.

Additional Resources

- **Splunk Docs: About Configuration Files:** https://docs.splunk.com/Documentation/Splunk/latest/Admin/Aboutconfigurationfiles
- **Splunk Docs: Configuration File Reference:** https://docs.splunk.com/Documentation/Splunk/latest/Admin/Configurationfilescatalog

Key Takeaways

- Configuration files are how you truly tailor Splunk to your specific needs.
- Start with changes through the web interface whenever possible for safety.
- Understand how configuration settings at different levels interact.

Up Next

In Part 2, we'll go deeper with practical examples of editing configuration files to achieve specific data parsing and transformation outcomes.

Configuration Chronicles: Unraveling Configuration File Essentials, Part 2

Objectives

- Practice modifying `props.conf` and `transforms.conf` for parsing and data manipulation.
- Learn how to troubleshoot issues with data onboarding and field extraction.
- Explore more advanced configuration techniques and best practices.

Scenario 1: Messy Web Server Logs

You're ingesting Apache-style access logs. Problem: events are one long line, making them hard to analyze. Goal: Extract fields like 'client IP', 'URL', 'timestamp'.

1. **Locate the Input:** In `inputs.conf`, find the stanza configuring this (e.g., [monitor:///var/log/apache/access.log])
2. **props.conf Time:** Create (if it doesn't exist) `props.conf` in your `system/local` directory, or ideally in a custom app's `local` folder.
3. **Define a Sourcetype:**

```
[sourcetype=apache_access]
EXTRACT-http_info = ^(?<clientip>\S+) \S+ \S+
\[(?<timestamp>[^]]+)\].*?
"(?<method>\S+)\s+(?<urlpath>\S+)\s+HTTP.*" (?<status>\d+)
TIME_FORMAT = %d/%b/%Y:%H:%M:%S
```

- ○ **Explanation:** Regex magic! This extracts your fields, and the TIME_FORMAT line ensures Splunk correctly interprets the timestamp.

Scenario 2: Enriching Data

You have firewall logs with source and destination IPs. You want a new field 'country' based on IP geolocation.

1. **Lookup Time:** [invalid URL removed] Requires a Lookup Definition and a CSV file mapping IPs to countries.
2. **transforms.conf:**

[firewall_geolookup]
external_cmd = geoiplookup clientip
fields_list = country

- ○ **Explanation:** We define a transform that calls an external script 'geoiplookup' (assumed to be set up). The results populate the 'country' field

Troubleshooting

- **No Data?:**
  - ○ Is the file path in inputs.conf correct?
  - ○ Are permissions right (can Splunk read the files)?
  - ○ Splunk's _internal index is your friend – look for errors there.
- **Wrong Fields:**
  - ○ Test in Splunk Web! Search bar lets you try regexes with rex
  - ○ Many online regex testers to help refine.
  - ○ Splunk community (https://answers.splunk.com/) is great for tricky parsing

Beyond the Basics

- **BREAK_ONLY_BEFORE / LINE_MERGER:** In `props.conf`, these help with multi-line events
- **calculated fields:** Create new fields at search time, e.g., | `eval bytes_per_second = bytes / duration`
- **REPORT-something:** `props.conf` settings for defining fields specifically visible in the Pivot
- **Conditional settings:** Apply configuration based on host, sourcetype…

Additional Tips

- **Small Changes, Restart Often:** Prevents huge debugging headaches.
- **Version Control:** Ideal for serious setups, but even a folder of 'config_backup_YYYYMMDD' is better than nothing.
- **Documentation:** Comments in your .conf files are lifesavers for future you!

Additional Resources

- **Splunk Docs: Common Regex Examples:** https://docs.splunk.com/Documentation/Splunk/latest/Knowledge/Usefieldextractions

Key Takeaways

- `props.conf` and `transforms.conf` are your data shaping powerhouses.
- Mastering regular expressions will make your configuration life much easier.
- Troubleshooting configuration issues requires a methodical approach.

Up Next

Splunk has several types of knowledge objects – lookup tables, event types, macros… Let's explore how they make your searches more efficient and powerful!

Knowledge Repository: Harnessing the Power of Knowledge Objects

Objectives

- Understand the different types of Splunk knowledge objects and their use cases.
- Learn how to create and manage lookups, event types, tags, and macros.
- Explore leveraging knowledge objects to power more efficient searches and dashboards.

Beyond Raw Data: Adding Context

Knowledge objects represent additional information you layer on top of your events, making them more meaningful for analysis. Let's break down the key types:

- **Lookups:**
  - Like spreadsheets uploaded to Splunk.
  - Map IP to country, user ID to full name, product code to description… you get the idea.
  - Use Cases: Data enrichment at search time.
- **Event Types:**
  - A way to categorize events.
  - Include search terms, tags, and colors.
  - Use Cases: Filter searches to specific errors, identify performance patterns in certain transaction types.
- **Tags:**
  - Simple key-value metadata added to events.
  - Unlike fields, they're NOT extracted automatically.
  - Use Cases: Group data from diverse sources ('web server'), mark sensitive data.

- **Macros:**
  - Reusable chunks of search logic
  - Can take arguments
  - Use Cases: Simplify complex searches, modularize dashboard logic so changes only need to be made in one place.

Scenario: Security Threat Analysis

1. **Bad IPs Lookup:** You have a CSV with known malicious IP addresses and their threat level (malware, phishing, etc.)
2. **"Suspicious Activity" Event Type:** Define one with a search identifying unusual login patterns, failed authentications, etc.
3. **"High-Risk Host" Tag:** Assign to servers based on their role or sensitivity
4. **Alerting Macro:** A reusable search chunk that takes a 'severity' argument, making your alerts more flexible.

Creating Knowledge Objects

- **Splunk Web:** The most user-friendly way. Look under the 'Settings' menu.
- **Configuration Files:** Can be trickier, but allows for bulk creation and automation.

Knowledge Objects in Action

- **Searches:**
  - ```
    lookup my_ip_lookup clientip OUTPUT
    threat_level
    ```
  - `eventtype=suspicious_activity`
  - `tag=high-risk_host`
- **Dashboards:** Panels can be driven by results of searches using knowledge objects, making them update dynamically as your data changes.
    ```

Additional Notes

- **Field Aliases:** Sometimes a simpler solution to relabel a field. Less powerful than lookups, but quick to set up.
- **Automatic Lookups:** Configured in `props.conf`, these are applied as events are ingested.
- **Permissions:** Control who can edit certain knowledge objects, especially sensitive ones.

Additional Resources

- **Splunk Docs: Lookups:** https://docs.splunk.com/Documentation/Splunk/latest/Knowledge/Lookupoverview
- **Splunk Docs: Other Knowledge Object Types:** https://docs.splunk.com/Documentation/Splunk/latest/Knowledge/Otherknowledgeobjecttypes

Key Takeaways

- Knowledge objects supercharge your Splunk data by adding context and categorization.
- They make building searches and dashboards easier, more consistent, and more adaptable.
- Consider your use cases carefully to choose the right type of knowledge object for each situation.

Up Next

Lookups deserve their own deep dive! Let's explore their configuration, use cases, and some advanced lookup techniques in the next chapter.

Lookup Labyrinth: Navigating Lookup Essentials, Part 1

Objectives

- Understand the core concepts behind lookups in Splunk.
- Learn how to create different types of lookup tables.
- Explore use cases for lookups to enrich and analyze your data.
- Master how to utilize lookups within searches.

Why Lookups Matter

- **Enhancing Data:** Add descriptive fields to cryptic codes or IDs. An IP address becomes a country name, a user ID becomes a full employee name...
- **Normalization:** Lookups can standardize inconsistent data. For example, mapping "USA", "United States", and "US" to a single value for cleaner analysis.
- **Performance:** For some tasks, lookups are more efficient than complex calculations or joins done at search time.

Lookup Basics

1. **Lookup Definition:**
   - Name: How you'll reference it in searches.
   - Type: CSV, geospatial lookup, scripted lookup (advanced!), etc.
2. **Lookup Table:** The data itself. This can be:
   - A manually uploaded CSV file.
   - An output from another Splunk search (results written to a lookup).
   - External sources through modular inputs (more advanced).

Scenario: Website Errors with Context

Your web access logs have HTTP Status Codes. Goal: Translate them into human-understandable messages AND categorize them.

CSV Lookup: http_statuses.csv

status_code, message, severity
200, OK, success
403, Forbidden, warning
404, Not Found, warning
500, Internal Server Error, error

...

Creating the Lookup (Splunk Web)

- **Settings -> Lookups -> Lookup Definitions**
- **New Lookup**
  - Name: 'http_status_lookup'
  - Filename: 'http_statuses.csv'
- **Save,** and Splunk will make it available for use.

The Magic: Using Your Lookup

sourcetype=web_access
| lookup http_status_lookup status_code OUTPUT message, severity

Now instead of just codes in your results, you have explanatory text!

Additional Features

- **Default Values:** What to do if a value ISN'T found in the lookup table?
- **Wildcards:** Matching can use *, e.g., your country lookup could match on partial IP prefixes for broader geolocating
- **Overwriting:** OUTPUTNEW to create a new field instead of overwriting an existing one with the same name.

Additional Resources

- **Splunk Docs: Create and Configure Lookups:**
  https://docs.splunk.com/Documentation/Splunk/latest/Knowl
  edge/Configurelookups
- **Splunk Docs: Use Lookups:**
  https://docs.splunk.com/Documentation/Splunk/latest/Searc
  hReference/Lookup

Key Takeaways

- Lookups are how you inject external context into your
  Splunk data.
- CSV lookups are the most common kind, but Splunk
  supports more dynamic types.
- The `lookup` command is your gateway to using the
  knowledge stored within a lookup table.

Up Next

Lookups can do even more! In Part 2, we'll explore automatic
lookups, advanced field manipulation techniques, and
performance considerations.

Lookup Labyrinth: Navigating Lookup Essentials, Part 2

Objectives

- Learn how to configure automatic lookups for data enrichment at indexing time.
- Discover techniques to work with multiple lookup values.
- Explore performance considerations when choosing between different lookup approaches.

Scenario: Proactive Threat Monitoring

You're ingesting firewall logs. Goal: Immediately flag events with IPs known to be malicious, and categorize the type of threat.

Automating with props.conf

In `props.conf` for your firewall sourcetype:

[sourcetype=firewall]
LOOKUP-bad_guys = threat_list_lookup clientip OUTPUT threat_type, severity

- **Result:** No need for the `lookup` command in searches! As events are ingested, Splunk does it for you!

When to Use Automatic Lookups

- **Critical Lookups:** If the lookup is essential to nearly all analysis of this data type, automatic makes sense.
- **Performance Sensitive:** Lookups at search time can add overhead. Automatic lookups shift the work to indexing. However…
- **Lookup Size & Changes:** Huge or frequently updated lookups might negatively impact indexing speed.

Many Matches: What Now?

Your IP lookup might have multiple entries per IP (different regions, severity, etc.).

- **MVOUTPUT:** `... OUTPUTNEW mv_threats AS threats`
  - Creates a multi-value field `threats`. Requires commands like `mvexpand` to use effectively.
- **Advanced:** Scripted Lookups can return complex data structures if you need truly custom handling.

Tradeoffs: Search-Time vs. Automatic

Approach	Pros	Cons
Search-Time Lookup ('lookup' command)	Flexible, change the lookup without re-indexing	Search performance overhead, less beginner-friendly
Automatic Lookup (in props.conf)	Efficient, fields available immediately	Changes require re-indexing, may impact indexer performance

Additional Optimization

- **Knowledge Bundle (Advanced):** For distributing lookups to forwarders to reduce network traffic.
- **Lookup Caching:** Lookups can be cached to speed up repeated lookups of the same values

Example: Putting it All Together

```
sourcetype=firewall threat_type=*
| stats count BY threat_type, severity, dest_ip
```

Imagine this without the automatic lookup – it'd be much less streamlined!

Additional Resources

- **Splunk Docs: Automatic Lookups:**
  https://docs.splunk.com/Documentation/Splunk/latest/Knowl edge/Automaticlookups
- **Splunk Docs: Performance Considerations with Lookups:**
  https://docs.splunk.com/Documentation/Splunk/latest/Knowl edge/Performanceconsiderationswithlookups

Key Takeaways

- Automatic lookups streamline analysis workflows and can improve performance for essential data enrichment.
- Splunk offers flexible ways to handle scenarios where a lookup might return multiple matching values.
- Carefully balance the convenience of automatic lookups against their potential effect on indexer resources.

Conclusion

Throughout this book, you have transformed from a curious beginner into a seasoned Splunk explorer. Let's recap the incredible ground you've covered:

- **Splunk's Role:** You understand how Splunk turns the chaos of machine data into actionable insights, empowering organizations to troubleshoot, optimize, and secure their systems.
- **Core Concepts:** Terms like indexes, events, fields, and search commands no longer hold any mystery. You architect effective data flows and wield configuration files to customize Splunk's behavior with precision.
- **Analysis Workflows:** From the initial search bar to stunning visualizations and proactive alerts, you craft end-to-end solutions that turn data into knowledge.
- **Advanced Techniques:** Knowledge objects, lookups, and even the ability to extend Splunk with custom scripting demonstrate the depth of the platform and the heights you've reached.

But This Isn't the End

The world of Splunk is constantly evolving! Here's how you can continue to grow your expertise:

- **Join the Community:** The Splunk community (especially Splunk Answers: https://answers.splunk.com/) is filled with veterans and newcomers alike. Share what you've learned, and get help overcoming your next challenge.
- **Splunk Apps:** Splunkbase: https://splunkbase.splunk.com/ contains a treasure trove of pre-built solutions. Explore, adapt, and find inspiration!

- **Explore Advanced Topics:** We lightly touched on things like distributed deployments, machine learning toolkits, and stream processing. Each of these could be a book in itself!

Unlocking Insights, One Search at a Time

Remember, Splunk is an incredible tool, but its true value lies in the questions **you** ask of your data. Each search you write has the potential to reveal:

- Hidden performance bottlenecks threatening your customers' experience.
- Security vulnerabilities that could have devastating consequences.
- Patterns in user behavior that drive new features and business growth.

The insights are out there. With your Splunk mastery, you have the power to uncover them. Go forth and analyze!

Final Tip: Splunk Docs (https://docs.splunk.com/) remains your most valuable reference. Bookmark it and don't hesitate to search it for detailed guidance as you tackle increasingly complex analysis challenges.

Congratulations on reaching this milestone. The world of data awaits your exploration!

---

www.ingramcontent.com/pod-product-compliance
Lightning Source LLC
LaVergne TN
LVHW081528050326
832903LV00025B/1674